Praise for

MY DAD'S A

MUSLIM

MY MOM'S A

LESBIAN

AND I'M A

LATTER-DAY SAINT

"I loved reading the book! I could have read it in one sitting if my schedule would have let me. It was funny, witty, honest, and intriguing."

—AL CARRAWAY, author of *More than the Tattooed Mormon* and keynote speaker

"Mike's story will leave you riveting for more, a true page-turner. His conviction, his faith, leaves you wanting to share his story with everyone."

—DENNIS SCHLEICHER, author of *Is He Nuts? Why a Gay Man Would Become a Member of the Church of Jesus Christ*

"We all wrestle with paradox in our personal faith and ideals. Can we love one who thinks differently than ourselves? Can relationships still exist when beliefs are not shared? Mike's story takes the reader through these difficult questions and lands us in a place of love, acceptance, and faith through fun, hard, and heart-changing stories."

—KURT FRANCOM, host of the *Leading Saints* podcast

MY DAD'S A

MUSLIM

MY MOM'S A

LESBIAN

AND I'M A

LATTER-DAY SAINT

MIKE RAMSEY

CFI

An imprint of Cedar Fort, Inc.
Springville, Utah

ISBN 13: 978-1-4621-3605-6

Published by CFI, an imprint of Cedar Fort, Inc.
2373 W. 700 S., Springville, UT 84663
Distributed by Cedar Fort, Inc., www.cedarfort.com

LIBRARY OF CONGRESS CATALOGING-IN-PUBLICATION DATA

Names: Ramsey, Mike, 1984- author.
Title: My dad's a Muslim, my mom's a lesbian, and I'm a member of the
    Church of Jesus Christ of Latter-day Saints / Mike Ramsey.
Description: [Springville, Utah] : CFI, An imprint of Cedar Fort, Inc.,
    [2019]
Identifiers: LCCN 2019012174 (print) | LCCN 2019022353 (ebook) | ISBN
    9781462136056 (perfect bound : alk. paper)
Subjects: LCSH: Ramsey, Mike, 1984- | Toleration. | Religious tolerance. |
    Mormons--Biography.
Classification: LCC BX8695 .R367 2019 (print) | LCC BX8695 (ebook) | DDC
    289.3092 [B]--dc23
LC record available at https://lccn.loc.gov/2019012174
LC ebook record available at https://lccn.loc.gov/2019022353

Cover design by Wes Wheeler
Cover design © 2019 by Cedar Fort, Inc.
Edited and typeset by Nicole Terry

Printed in the United States of America

10 9 8 7 6 5 4 3 2 1

Printed on acid-free paper

To those who are different.
Share your story.

CONTENTS

PROLOGUE

A FEW YEARS AGO, I WAS having a wonderfully pointless conversation with two friends when one of them cocked his head up and said, "I've decided I'm pretty special. I had an open-heart surgery on my enlarged aorta. That makes me one in fifty thousand."

Not wanting to be outdone, my other friend lifted his eyebrows the way a professor tends to do before saying something profound and slowly said, "You know, I have Marcus Gunn Jaw Winking Syndrome. I literally wink whenever I bite down. That makes me one in ten million."

As I thought about their uniqueness, I scrambled through my oddities trying to think of what I could say that would be relevant to this new conversation of one-upping that we had ventured upon. Beating one in ten million wasn't going to be easy. Then, as nonchalant as a lion preparing to pounce on a gazelle, I shared three true things about myself.

"My dad's a Muslim, my mom's a lesbian, and I'm a Mormon. I'm pretty sure that makes me roughly one in 7.4 billion."

The room fell deathly silent. Both of my friends' jaws dropped as they stared at me for what seemed like an eternity. Then, all at once, we began to laugh hysterically. I don't know why we laughed. The sensational statement might have come out like an extremely well-executed joke, but the reality of the situation is that it's my life.

I hadn't put the words Muslim, lesbian, and Mormon—or rather, member of The Church of Jesus Christ of Latter-day Saints—together in a single statement before, and it made me realize just how unique it was and how interested others were to hear about it. As the days, months, and years went on, I realized that the life I've lived has been anything but normal. Instead, my life to this point seems to have all the elements that a decently entertaining story needs: despair, comedy, failure, wonder, and success. So, I decided it was high time to write it down.

Now that I think about it, the driving force that ties everything in my story together is the struggle for understanding. That seems like as good of a place to start as any.

Let's begin with struggle.

CHAPTER 1

In the Beginning,
There Was Struggle

I WAS A THIRTY-YEAR-OLD DAD DOING my best to keep one of my daughters from falling into the water while sitting on a bumpy blue boat as it rolled through room after room. Dancing dolls that sang "It's a Small World" went from being cute to completely distracting as my phone buzzed in my pocket. Initially I had planned on ignoring it, thinking it was a work email that my director of operations could handle, but against my better judgment, I reached in my pocket with one hand while my other was busy keeping little hands and feet in the boat at all times. As the screen lit up, I stared long and hard at the message I never thought I would see. Of course, it would make sense to receive this message while being at the most magical place on earth.

"Email from Sied."

This would be the first time in my life I had ever heard from my father.

/ / / / /

Let's not get too ahead of ourselves. This story starts long before, and one must hear the entirety of it in order to appreciate that moment at Disneyland in 2014. I want to tell you about the beginning—actually, even before the beginning—and explain how I came to be in the first place.

My mom left the confines of her strict upbringing as the only girl, with five older brothers, to go to college at Utah State University in 1983. With the move, she finally felt free to "let loose" without facing the constant lectures from her Latter-day Saint father that made up the majority of their relationship during her childhood in Burley.

Burley's a small town of ten thousand along the Snake River in Southern Idaho. Most of the area was farms, the rest was factories. There were more cows in the locality than people. It is the type of town that folks dream of escaping from, especially my mom, but always seem to end up going back to. Some by choice, most by destiny or default.

Churches dotted most street corners, and the leftover corners ended up with bars. If you didn't go to church on Sunday, you went to the bar. If you did both, either you were Catholic or you hoped neither of the groups would find out about each other. If you didn't do either, it would be a hard place to have any type of group. My mom tried both and didn't like either of the street corner options. She simply didn't fit anywhere.

Her memories of attending The Church of Jesus Christ of Latter-day Saints as a teen consisted of dos and do nots with very little talk of love or the Savior. I don't know if it was due to only paying attention to things that bugged her or if her leaders were focused more on the cultural side of how to be a Latter-day Saint and less on how to be like the Savior. Either way, she saw youth her age act a certain way at church and a very different way at school. It always bothered her. Ultimately, from her perspective, she never could see past what she considered to be hypocrisy at church and tended to find kindness and spirituality outside of the chapel and very much on her own.

From the stories I have heard, the culminating experience that pushed her away was a conversation with her bishop (the volunteer church leader over the congregation).

He called her in for an interview about how she was doing. She felt uncomfortable talking to him—largely due to her complete and utter distrust for men in positions of power—and decided that he needed to promise that if she told him things in confidence then he wouldn't share them with her parents. According to her, he agreed with a trusting smile and coaxed her to continue with her story. After my mom spilled the beans about all the shenanigans that she got up to as a slightly rebellious adolescent, the bishop said all would be fine but then went right to her father. So by the time she meandered home, there was a cold chair and a stern voice waiting for her, which led to a multiple-hour lecture about how her life wouldn't amount to much and she was headed for a premature pregnancy and homelessness unless she straightened up and started paying attention in church. Of course, that didn't sit well with her, as she felt no love, no forgiveness, and definitely no trust. Her mind was made up to find a different path, though her next wouldn't bear any better fruit.

I will always remember her explanation of the "underage bar crowd" in Burley. She told me they would accept anyone—well, as long as you smoked, drank, and tried whatever drugs were around. The thought of new and accepting friends allured her, and she dove in head first only to find the same hypocrisy, where friendship and kindness were always based on the condition of doing what others told her to do.

She simply longed for people who could love and accept her for who she was. She wanted to be around people who were kind. Overall, many of her teenage years were spent being let down on that front, and the thought of a new and bigger college town away from religion and the opinions of others offered her a fresh start to find herself. So when the opportunity came to head to Utah State, she couldn't have been more excited.

My mom had a hidden beauty about her that was covered by big glasses and an extremely shy personality. As people came to truly know her, though, they were met with a very strong-willed and fun woman who preferred sports over singing and would rather visit a dentist than be caught dead in a dress.

She liked to "hang" in the student rec building and shark the pool table. She was good—so good that a chunk of the Utah State football team would line up to play her on days off. She would beat them one by one while they laughed at each other and watched in amazement.

That situation might be as intimidating as being a bull-fighting matador for some women, but my mom's five older brothers had taught her long ago how to compete fiercely in everything she did. Some of her favorite moments were beating her brothers at various sports against all odds, though she knew the real "beating" would come from them later.

There was another group that liked to hang out in the rec building as well. They were international students from Palestine who found themselves in Utah looking for good education and great women. One, in particular, had his eye on my mom. He showered her with gifts and compliments constantly. He told her stories of life in a war zone and his struggle to live as a Muslim in the land of Jews. It struck a chord. Knowing her, I doubt that did much for helping him win a game of nine-ball, but it did win over her heart. My mom wasn't used to the middle-eastern hospitality that suitors crafted for the chance to find a woman. She'd had such bad experiences with boys in Burley that the stark difference was a complete breath of fresh air. But, like much of her childhood spent trying to find her place, things weren't exactly as they seemed.

I don't know many of the details about my parents' courtship, mainly because my dad wasn't a subject that we talked about as I was growing up. I had one picture of him, and before I was eight, I ripped it up.

I honestly can't remember why I tore the picture up. I still see the sepia-toned shot and his dark glasses above a thick mustache in my mind as my little hands tore again and again. I just can't remember the motive. When my mom found the pieces lying on the floor, she took it as a sign that he wasn't up for discussion, so that was that.

The one thing I did know was that their relationship obviously and most definitely did not work out.

My parents' relationship became strained; she distanced herself, and he overcompensated with extreme possessiveness and anger. From the bits and pieces I've gathered over the years, there were plenty of reasons that the strain took place. One stood out head and shoulders above the rest.

My mom developed stronger feelings for one of her professors than for my dad. That professor happened to be a woman. My mom said that even from a young age she looked at women a little differently than she thought she should. This time the feelings were too strong and too confusing to ignore. Her professor was smart, funny, and sporty and seemed to pay particularly close attention to my mom. The complications were plentiful, but my mom made the decision to do what she could to spend as much time with her professor as possible and avoid my dad. To make matters more complicated, she discovered that she was pregnant with me shortly after breaking up with my father.

I like to consider this her "hat trick" moment in life—three major events emerging at the same time that would have caused any other woman to crumble. She finally accepted the realization that she had much stronger feelings for women than men, broke up with her serious boyfriend, and discovered that she was pregnant all at the same time. I wouldn't wish that combination of events on anyone, and yet she was in the middle of dealing with those things and trying to make sense of it all.

While many would have recommended abortion as her only option, that thought didn't settle well with her—or me, as I sit here thinking that my whole existence might not have been—and she opted to carry on. As I have tried to understand that time of her life, I have come to the conclusion that there is no combination of words that could adequately explain the confusion and difficulty she was facing. In the midst of it, she decided to keep the pregnancy a secret from my father and fled back to her hometown to give birth.

There was a mix of reasons my mom has shared with me over the years for why she kept the pregnancy secret. Most of them were centered on the fact that when she discovered her pregnancy, she was scared of my father, his cultural views of women, and his religion. When she started to spend less time with him, he compensated by showing up at her apartment unannounced and questioning her roommates and even her professor about her whereabouts. She was nervous that if he found out she was pregnant, and they weren't together, he might try to claim the right to her child, steal me, and flee to the Middle East, where she would have no right to bring me back home. While I have no idea if this was a likely scenario, she was definitely scared enough to go to extreme measures to ensure the pregnancy stayed a secret.

As soon as the news of the untimely "baby bump" rolled its way through her brothers and parents upon her arrival back in Burley, it became their turn to offer up advice on what she should do. Most told her that she wasn't ready for a child and that adoption was the only option, and religion was the only way to make amends. Yet again, and with firmer resolve, she resisted and let it be known that she was going to keep the baby and do the best she could on her own.

/////

I was born on June 30, 1984, at Cassia Regional Hospital in good ol' Burley, Idaho. It happened to be the day that the Olympic torch came through the town on its way to the summer games in Los Angeles. Everyone told my mom it was a sign of great things for me since *nothing* of significance came through Burley other than constant high winds and the occasional snowstorm.

Though my grandparents had struggled with my mom's decision-making for years, they were always very supportive in their actions. If my mom was willing to bear a lecture, then they would pitch in and help her any way they could after the fact. My birth was no different. They were not happy with my mom being pregnant. It was very much against their personal moral code. Nonetheless, they stood by her choice to keep me and offered a helping hand even when some told them that they should let my mom fend for herself.

According to my grandpa, who was in the room when I was born, I had big outstretched hands as I let out my first screams. He thought I would be great at sports while my grandma thought I would be great at piano. I ended up mediocre at both, so they could each be half right, and I could be half good at two things you need to be great at to attract womanly attention and manly respect—or at least so I thought through most of my adolescence.

My mom had a couple of semesters left to complete when I was born, and she knew that my father would still be at Utah State. Considering the secret birth and wanting to keep things from getting seriously complicated, she made the hard decision for me to stay in Burley with my grandparents until she finished her degree to become a special education teacher.

The young, carefree girl who spent her time on the pool tables of the rec building gave way to a single mother who was determined to graduate as fast as possible in order to make a life for her son. She told me it was one of the hardest times of her life. She would speed home on Friday after classes jamming out to Kansas's "Carry On Wayward Son" and then cry for the entire two-and-a-half-hour drive back to Utah State on Sundays.

Meanwhile, I got chubby under my grandparents' care, and according to anonymous sources, I would sit on everyone's lap, grab their ears, and suck on their chin. This is not a habit I have kept intact.

After my mom finished school against the odds, she took a teaching job in Utah, and we moved into our first place together. It was a dark basement apartment with concrete floors and lawn chairs for furniture. Though the memories are few and far between, I do remember standing at the top of the stairs to our apartment as someone was showing my mom how to swing a golf club. I stepped forward at the exact wrong time and took the backswing to the face and proceeded to fall down the stairs. I sure wish I could have gotten ahold of their ears and let their chin know who was boss.

Another memory comes from a tape recording my mom kept over the years. I never wanted to go to bed (imagine that). So I would try to tell my mom stories to postpone the inevitable, and my favorite was *The Big Bad "Woof."*

She would try to put me down, and I would say, "Mom, the big bad woof is huffing."

"It's time for bed, Mike."

"But he'll blow our house down!"

"It's still time for bed."

"No! Three piggies have to get away."

Needless to say, my story didn't work and I had to go to bed. As I got older, if I was ever trying to put something off, she would remind me of the "woof" and how she always wins in the end.

Over the next few years, we moved from Salt Lake City to American Falls and then to Pocatello, Idaho. The time was filled with Ninja Turtles action figures, lots of TV, and very few friends. It's a period of my life that I can't say I enjoyed. While most boys my age were playing with their fathers, I was getting acquainted with the comforts of a TV in a lonely room. The neighborhoods we lived in weren't safe enough for an adult to be alone outside, let alone a child, so instead of roaming the neighborhood with kids my age, I learned to entertain myself indoors.

My mom worked extremely hard during the day with very demanding high school kids who hadn't had a fair hand dealt to them. She taught kids who had dyslexia, Down syndrome, autism, fetal alcohol syndrome, and everything else you could imagine. Then she came home in the evenings to a never-ending list of demands from me. She had no breaks, no social life, and no hope that her future would bring her anything beyond the life of struggle that we lived. But through it all, she always greeted me with a smile on her face. My mom was my best friend.

I did have a few other childhood friends, but I grew up a little too quickly from the influence they had on me. For instance, at a daycare in American Falls, one of my friends said it would be really fun to call our sitter a name. He told me how to spell it and said I should repeat the word over and over. So, with all the bravery a young five-year-old could muster, I stood up amongst a crowd of my peers playing with blocks and blankies and shouted, "Hey, lady! You're a [bleep]." The actual word I spelled out rhymed with Lilo's alien friend Stitch, but like Disney, I want to keep things PG.

I had no idea what the word meant, but her gasp and the look on her face led me to think that it probably wasn't a great oration of her beauty and ability with children. I did, however, find out that I preferred the taste of Irish Spring soap to Dial.

I wish I could say that bad words were the worst things I learned from friends. That sadly wasn't the case. My best friend started smoking cigarettes when he was seven and would want to play with me for an excuse to smoke outside in our fort. I hated that he smoked. I hated it because my mom did too, and it stunk and made me cough. My friend, in his best grown-up voice, told me that he was addicted and that I shouldn't start up or I would end up like him. While I was grateful for the sound advice, it didn't stop him from offering, nor did it stop my constant rejections.

That just scratches the surface of the situations I was in at way too young of an age. The bad thing about bad neighborhoods is that there is no end to issues unleashed on the inhabitants, and children are usually the ones who take the brunt of it. While I wish I could say otherwise, I didn't escape unscathed.

One day, while I was walking home from school in Pocatello, an old van started to follow close behind me. I turned to see who it was, but the driver had sunglasses and a hat on. I walked a little faster. The van kept up the pace and began to close in on me. Eventually it was to my side, and I stopped. The man in the car looked at me and reached to grab something. Everything inside my little body felt sick, and I could only think of one thing to do. Run!

I ran as fast as I had ever run before through the remaining four zigzagging blocks to my house. The van followed, but on the last turn, I gained distance and hurried through the front door. I could hardly breathe as I imagined some snatcher outside looking for a way into the house. As I sat there waiting for my mom to come home, I realized how much I hated where we lived, and I desperately hoped that we wouldn't be there much longer. A week later, a child disappeared not far from where we lived.

My younger years were slow, hard, and filled with memories I would rather forget than replay to write this book. There was one bright and constant light in my life during those times: my mom, and the love she had for me. For a third-grader, that was all that mattered.

CHAPTER 2

When Being Gay Didn't Mean Being Happy

DURING SUMMERS AND WEEKENDS, IT SEEMED more often than not we ended up at my grandma and grandpa's home in good ol' Burley, Idaho. I absolutely loved to visit them, and my mom tolerated it for my sake. They had a big white brick house with a trampoline, lots of grass, and a cow-filled pasture in the backyard.

My grandma would make the best home-cooked meals, and she always had a few cookies stashed away for me somewhere in the house and was more than willing to let me eat more than one if I asked nicely.

My grandpa had a woodworking shop, where he spent hours on warm days making all types of things. If I begged, and sweetened the deal with some weed pulling, he would make me random wooden toys. My favorite was an exact replica—bit of an exaggeration here—AK-47 assault rifle from Jurassic Park. He even carved the JP logo into it! I spent hours roaming around the overgrown pasture causing the extinction of at least thirty species of make-believe dinosaurs with that gun. The same amount of time was probably spent cleaning carpets from the mud and manure I tracked through the house.

To my excitement, after my third-grade year of school in Pocatello and the close call with the kid snatcher, along with my mom's failing health due to severe neck and back pain, my mom accepted a teaching position in Burley and we moved in with my grandparents.

After years of running from her family and hometown, it seemed like the universe conspired to bring my mom back to her home. There is no doubt the move was largely for my sake, another sacrifice she made to ensure I had the best chance to succeed. Also, my mom was prepping for a series of surgeries, and she needed someone to care for her. I would have, but my cooking consisted of bowls of cereal and toasted bread, which wouldn't have given her the nutrients she needed. She said she knew the move home was right, but I know it was hard for her to come back to the town where she didn't fit in.

As for me, I honestly couldn't have been more excited! I had all the people I truly loved under one roof and had just gone from a four-hundred-square-foot apartment to a five-bedroom country house with all the country fixings. For a nine-year-old boy, I felt like my fortunes had finally changed, and I was on top of my new world with nothing but clear skies ahead.

That's when a conversation happened that changed everything.

It was our first winter in Burley. My grandparents had taken their usual post-Christmas retreat to St. George, Utah, which left the entire house to my mom and me for a couple of months.

I remember sitting at the kitchen counter eating dinner one winter night when my mom told me she had something important to discuss. I knew whatever was coming had to be big because we always watched TV when we ate. Always. So for the TV to be off, I figured I must have been in some serious trouble, and I started to run through all my secrets that might have gotten out. Did she see the dirty clothes I stuffed under the bed? Or did she find out about me talking a little too much in class the other day? I also thought through my last trip to the bathroom and tried to remember if I left the toilet seat up, and then I remembered that I didn't pick it up at all, which probably meant the seat got sprinkled. That had to be it!

As I prepped for the lecture I had grown accustomed to about bathroom courtesy, I realized something was off. My mom didn't look mad. She looked concerned. After what seemed like a lifetime of hesitation, and with a very worried look on her face, she looked at me with tears welling up in her eyes and said, "I'm gay."

All of my hidden secrets combined didn't seem like a blip on the radar compared to the bomb my mom just dropped. Honestly, I wasn't even fully sure I knew what being gay meant. I knew at recess kids would call someone "gay" as an insult and that it meant my mom didn't like men. But that was the extent.

I looked at her and burst into tears.

I have no idea why I cried. I didn't understand why this revelation about my mom hurt me so much. At that time, I had no concept of it being wrong or right, but I just knew that things were going to change, and that scared me.

The next day, I woke up and tried to act like nothing had happened. My mom asked me if I was okay on the way to school, and I assured her I was fine, but deep down I was battling how to respond to the news. Was I supposed to be happy? Sad? Should I treat my mom differently? Should I talk to her about it? Should I talk to someone else about it? Does this make my mom a bad person? Is she going to go to jail? Does this mean I am going to be like her?

The questions seemed to bounce around my head like a blind-folded bull in a very small china closet as I made my way through the halls and sat at my desk. I had no idea how to frame what had just happened and desperately wanted to find understanding.

The bell rang, which brought my attention back to the Idaho history lesson that had just started. I figured I could forget about everything and just focus on the class. Within the first few minutes I put my head in my arms, and my teacher's words became more and more distant. I couldn't stop playing that moment from the night before over and over in my head.

"I'm gay."

The tear-filled look on her face seared itself into every thought and feeling that was running through my little body.

Then, I sobbed uncontrollably while sitting at my desk in the middle of the lesson. Full alligator tears and moans, which wasn't generally the cool thing to do in the middle of a fourth-grade class. To this day, it's the hardest I have ever cried in public.

The teacher took me out into the hall and repeatedly asked me what was wrong. I had no idea what to say. I didn't know if I could say anything. It was the nineties in rural southern Idaho. Through gasps for breath and with tears still rolling down my cheeks I simply said, "My mom told me that she's gay."

The look on the teacher's face went blank, and I could tell she had no idea how to respond. She just stared at me in silence, taking the time to process what I had just told her, and said that I had better go with her to the principal's office.

Did this mean that my mom was in trouble? Were they going to take me away from her? The questions continued to pile up into an ever-growing mound of confusion.

The talk with the principal was short and simple. With deep concern in her eyes, she told me she knew my mom and not to worry. She told me that she was sorry I was sad but that my mom was a good person. Those simple words relieved me more than I could have imagined. My darkest fears subsided considerably when I knew that this wasn't something that would separate me from her.

Looking back, I couldn't imagine the damage that the wrong words could have caused at that time. I had no idea who to trust or talk to, but a school principal seemed like the smartest person on earth to me, and I trusted her words. The responsibility our words carry to children is not something to be taken lightly, and I will be forever grateful for a wise leader that day.

A call was made to my mom at the junior high to come pick me up. She rushed over to my school as fast as she could and surely feared the worst. After all, she had just started as the department head of the special education program and only had three months in the position. If news got out that she was a lesbian, she worried the district might not extend her teaching contract beyond the first year.

By the time she reached my school, her eyes were already red with tears as she, the principal, and my teacher talked for what seemed like hours in the office while I waited in the foyer.

When my mom came out, she thanked the two ladies for how they handled the situation, and we started the drive home. She was crying and said that they all had decided the best thing to do was to keep it all a secret. She told me I had to be much more careful about who I told and warned me that most people didn't understand what it meant to be gay and that it could lead to bad things happening if the wrong people knew.

She dropped me off at home and made her way back to finish out her day of classes at the junior high. I lay down on the floor in my grandpa's office and stared at the ceiling. I was unable to move and just looked straight up for what seemed like an eternity.

The longer I stared, the angrier I became. Instead of the questions based on fear that had completely filled my mind over the past twenty-four hours, I settled on one question with all my energy.

Why?

Why was my mom gay? Why was she like that? Why wasn't someone else's mom gay instead of mine? Why didn't I have a dad? Would this mean I would have another mom? Why? Why? Why? Why? Why! It just didn't seem fair, and the more I thought about it, the more my thoughts turned to God.

I remember always believing in God. We didn't go to church very often unless my grandparents snagged us for special events, but my mom always talked about spirituality, and she had shown me that she believed in some type of higher power.

I believed in Him that day as well. I came to the conclusion that I didn't like Him very much.

With tears in my eyes, I shouted at heaven with all the animosity a nine-year-old could muster and blamed everything I possibly could on God that day. It was His fault that I didn't have a dad—and would never, given that my mom didn't like men. It was His fault that my life was so hard.

That night when my mom came home, she made dinner and asked if I was okay. I replayed the vision of lying on the floor in my bitterness, unable to make sense of the world around me. I wanted to say no and burst into tears again. Instead, I said yes. We flipped on the TV and watched while we ate.

I have often wondered why my mom felt the need to tell me when she did. I was barely old enough to notice girls and realize that I actually might like them. After our talk, I didn't know what to think.

She told my grandma and grandpa shortly before she told me. My grandma never gave her opinion, and I'm sure my grandpa gave a lecture about the need for my mom to go to church and find a good man. But once they knew, they just acted like my mom hadn't told them anything and did their best to keep her in the closet. But she was ready to embrace her sexuality. She had been living day to day for so long that it wasn't a possibility for her to think about her future as a lesbian until we were cared for under my grandparents' roof and she had time to simply be herself.

After she came out, it didn't initially change anything about our way of life. I went through the stages of grief in private and did my best to not talk to anyone about how I was feeling, or why I was feeling grief in the first place.

For my mom, the biggest change that occurred was that she was finally set free. She had been single for ten years and was done with being alone. Later in life, she told me that when I was a toddler she saw a lesbian couple in the store and just followed them around from aisle to aisle. Not willing to approach them, but just longing for people who understood how she felt. Her loneliness as a single parent in southern Idaho was hard enough; to add on top the feelings she had for women put her in a league of her own. One thing was for sure now: the time of keeping secrets and being alone was over for her.

After the winter, she started going out on the weekends while I would stay home with my grandparents. It wasn't too often at first, but over time it became more and more common that her nights were busy and her weekends were completely booked with new friends.

For her, it was what she needed in order to find herself and where she fit. For me, it felt like waiting endlessly at a stoplight for things to get back to normal so we could continue with how things used to be. I had always been with my mom. She was my best friend and we did everything together. That was all about to change.

/////

I don't remember the first time I met Tina. I just know that my mom was serious about her. More so than her other girlfriends that she had spent time around. Tina had grown up in a nearby town in a big Latter-day Saint family, very similar to my mom's experience. She was a few years younger with curly hair and a big smile. She liked to joke and tease in a way that ensured you knew she meant no harm and was simply trying to break the ice. She was soft-spoken and shy in crowds but had a much larger friend network than my mom and always had somewhere to meet someone for lunch or an evening out. Tina had the social life that my mom longed for but had sacrificed for years as she was raising me.

Tina had gone to the Church-run Ricks College after graduating from high school in the super small town of Oakley, Idaho, and then she ran off to San Francisco with a roommate to pursue a gay lifestyle. She had spent years without contacting her family and had fallen into some extremely serious drug addictions that were her way of coping with life. By the time my mom had met her, Tina had been sober for years and was very involved in Narcotics Anonymous. I respected that. She also convinced my mom to stop smoking and drinking, which I also really liked.

Some of my first memories of Tina were actually on NA campouts that she brought us on. I can tell you that I sure got quite the education sitting around campfires hearing some of the craziest stories about where drug addictions had led different people. It made it extremely easy for me to make up my mind that I would never in a thousand years try drugs.

I remember when we moved out of my grandparents' and in with Tina. She had a basement apartment on Conant Street in Burley, Idaho. Yep, we were back to a basement apartment. There was a combined living room and kitchen with dark wood paneling on the walls that rocked the '70s better than bellbottoms and headbands.

It was small, it was dark, and it was hard. The neighborhood was bad. I've already discussed bad neighborhoods, so suffice it to say that I hated my time there. Though Tina and my mom did their best to make it comfortable, I just couldn't come to terms with the whole situation. I loved my grandparents and missed them dearly. I missed the food. I missed being able to have friends over and feel comfortable. Overall, I was secretly bitter and way too embarrassed to enjoy this new member of our household. It was simply too complicated for my mind to make sense of, and I had no idea what our new normal was supposed to be.

Around that same time, Tina and my mom planned a ceremony. It wouldn't be legal according to the state of Idaho, but that didn't matter to them. On a Friday night in the old schoolhouse in Oakley, they had a secret wedding with close friends. I don't think any family members came but me. I am honestly not even sure if either of their families knew about it. I was twelve years old and very confused about everything. I looked around the decorated room. There were stacks of rainbow-colored presents piled higher than me. A live band was playing the greatest mix of country songs southern Idaho could muster for what might have been one of the first big gay ceremonies in the state. As the music rang through my ears, I realized something that has stuck with me over the years. I was the only kid at the ceremony.

The room was filled with men and women who had made a decision on how they felt about homosexuality and this couple getting married. I sat there not knowing where I stood on anything. I didn't know if I should smile or cry.

My mom looked so happy. She seemed complete as she sat in a room full of people celebrating. She had found the love of her life and her future had never looked brighter, and because of that I was happy for her. On the other hand, I had found the dessert table and decided that instead of trying to process everything, my future would include a piece of cake. As I ate, my mind began to wonder if the person who baked it knew it was for a lesbian ceremony. Would they have refused if they had known? Would they tell people that my mom was gay? Would the word get to kids at school? Or did my moms have to lie about who the cake was for so they could have one for the celebration?

I didn't ask anyone those questions. I didn't talk with anyone about my mom being a "just-married" lesbian, and I don't remember anyone talking to me. It was just one of those things that wasn't brought up. Not by my mom, not by Tina, and not by my grandparents or any other family members. Everyone just referred to Tina, her partner, as my mom's "friend" at events and family gatherings, and the big rainbow-colored elephant in the room was never discussed.

So, how was it to actually be raised by a lesbian couple in Southern Idaho? Well, first off, the area is extremely conservative and equally religious, which led to me feeling very self-conscious about the situation. I always felt a certain amount of pity or bridled curiosity from onlookers. I imagined that when I left the room people would mention something. Especially with adults. Occasionally, a well-meaning lady or two would pull me aside and say, "I think you are just a very special kid and have just done so well, considering . . . everything."

Ultimately, I don't think people knew how to respond to the situation because they had no frame of reference or other examples to draw from. I was the first child being raised by a gay couple they knew. That still holds true for many all these years later.

I think it is also important to note that for an only child that spent the first ten years with a single mom, being raised by two moms was very comparable to growing up with any other step-parent plus a few . . . quirks.

Initially, it was hard to share my mom's time with someone else who had different ideas and rules on how I should be raised. That's just a normal struggle of blended families. Given that deep down I simply wanted a father figure and didn't know how to feel about homosexuality in general, I struggled getting along with both of my moms more than I should have. You could call it a passive-aggressive protest of sorts. They truly did their best, but it was like trying to run a marathon through a muddy bog with no directions, which led to a lot of dead ends and sticky situations.

I had two parents but no dad at home. I taught myself to shave, I had to be the muscle around the house, and I had to be on my own team when we played Battle of the Sexes. Okay, we didn't play that game, but if we had, it would have been an unfair advantage on the side of the ladies. Especially because all of our dogs were female as well, so I was really a lone man in the wilderness.

I basically learned to be very comfortable around women but was extremely intimidated around most men. I didn't trust them. I didn't know how to act or talk to "dads" as an adolescent and largely avoided it. I longed for fatherly figures but put up a wall against most that tried. I loved but feared my grandpa for no apparent reason. I never knew quite how to act around my five uncles.

When it came to friends, I never brought up my moms' relationship, and I don't think they really had the courage to ask. I avoided bringing friends over to my house at all costs to avoid awkward situations. I remember one friend who did come over and stay the night when we were about thirteen. He said, "So, your mom sleeps in that bedroom, but where does her roommate sleep?"

I looked at him for a minute, not knowing how to answer the question, and did what any thirteen-year-old put in the same situation would do. I lied through my teeth. I said that there were two rooms on that side of the house. Then we went back to playing the video game we were half-heartedly into, and no more was said.

Family gatherings were also quite the experience. Some of mom's brothers weren't very warm and accepting of Tina at first. When my mom came out of the closet, she had visits from a few of them where they let it be known that they didn't support what she was doing. Some at least told her that they loved her. I know it still hurt my mom dearly, but over the years most have been much more inviting and kind.

After my mom and Tina had been together for a couple of years, we had an extended family trip planned to the Flyin' B Ranch in central Idaho, which was the highlight on all of our calendars. My grandpa's business, a heating and electric company, would pay a certain part of the way each year and each person had to come up with minimal funding. It had become a yearly tradition that kept the Ramseys close.

My mom asked if Tina could come, and after the extended family had a meeting about it, she was told no. Eventually, my grandpa even offered to pay for Tina's ticket and tried to convince his children that it would be the right thing to do but was still turned down.

I can't tell you how bad that hurt my moms. We didn't do much with the Ramsey clan for a long time after that.

In contrast, Tina's family always had an invitation open for us. We were invited to every family event and were expected to be there. My mom felt more comfortable with them than with her own siblings. Tina's parents provided me the same gifts that the other grandkids got on birthdays and holidays and always tried to show me as much love as they could.

It wasn't ever easy. I was a stepchild and had missed twelve years of Tina's nieces and nephews playing games at Grandma's and having group sleepovers, but I felt welcome. I didn't know exactly what to call them and would get asked often, "How are you related to them?" I would stumble through an answer that made the poor questioner and me squirm in our boots and look for any reason to change the subject.

Looking back and seeing the contrast of how the two families reacted has been a great lesson in my life. Both families had a patriarch and matriarch that were Latter-day Saints and both families resided in Southern Idaho, yet each group handled things so differently. Tina's family was instantly supportive in including us. The Ramseys started out very cold toward my mom's announcement and partner, but over the years almost everyone warmed up to Tina. It just took a lot more time and hurt to get there. Years after the first rejection, Tina was invited to Flyin' B Ranch and had a wonderful time. She even made it into the family photo at the ranch standing right by my mom.

Years later I heard a story about Tina's mother that helped me understand a choice she made that led to the difference between the two families' initial reactions. Tina's family had been through a lot. The oldest daughter had gotten pregnant in high school. Tina had run off from Ricks College with a woman to San Francisco. A son had come home from a mission for the Church and was completely done with religion. Another son's wife ran off and left him raising two girls on his own. The list of parental woes goes on with challenges that you would never want to see your children face. At some point along the way, Tina's mom had all that she could bear and met with the Apostle David B. Haight, who was a senior leader of the Church and happened to live in Oakley, Idaho, as well. After she explained what was happening with all the children and wondered desperately what she could do, he simply told her to love them . . . no matter what.

She took the advice to heart, and the love that she and her husband showed trickled down through everyone in the family. They taught by example that no matter the trials each person had to face, the family would answer with love. It's not uncommon to be at a family reunion and one minute the grandparents share a quick prayer or spiritual thought, and in the next some of the family members are cracking open cans of Bud Lights while others drink root beer, and all can enjoy conversations around the campfire in perfect harmony. While I now understand more, I didn't always. As a teenager, the phrase "perfect harmony" was far from words that mingled themselves into my vocabulary.

Around the middle of junior high, it seemed impossible to get through a full day without a big argument with my mom and Tina over chores, grades, attitude, or any of the other countless things that mothers and sons could argue about. Undealt-with frustration seemed to build inside me like a brewing volcano ready to explode at a moment's notice. I wanted out. I wanted a break from the feelings of being so different and secretive. Ultimately, I wanted to be someone else, somewhere else, with a different family, and I had no idea how to let my raw thoughts and feelings be known.

Several years later, I actually wrote a story called *Reflection* about a few of these junior high and high school experiences that I would like to share about this time in my life.

/ / / / /

"Reflection"
For BYU–Idaho English 111

My mother is not as beautiful as a lake.
Most of the time she is calm,
But when the winds of her anger blow she becomes fierce
And her waves crash down with ferocious power.
She is deep and unclear.
The sun does not glisten off her face,
But when I look at my mother I see my reflection staring right
back at me.

A poem can reveal more about a person than a person can reveal
about themselves. At least, that is my opinion. And that was my poem
about the person that I have shared a relationship with for my entire
life. Her name is Janet and she doesn't have a middle name. My
relationship with my mother is much like the weather in Rexburg,
Idaho. Clear and sunny, but on a second's notice all hell could break
loose.

I remember last spring break, my senior year in high school, the
weather in Idaho was cold enough to make my dog yelp every time
she went outside to do her business. My mom and I decided that we
should take a family trip to the "most magical place on earth," so we
went to Las Vegas.

My mom and I had not been on a family trip since I was ten years
old, so when we decided to go, both of us were inevitably excited. I
remember sitting with her in the computer room looking at the nine-
teen-inch monitor that was big enough even my mom could read.
We compared plane tickets, looked up hotels, reviewed articles on the
entertainment, and even drooled over the cherry-red Dodge Viper on
Vegascarsforyou.com. Finally, everything was in order, so we packed
up and set off on our way to Sin City.

Vegas was amazing in every way. The lights, the cars, the shows; there was so much to do and see, I found my heart racing with my feet to each new thing with the look of a six-year-old's big eyes and dumbfounded excitement. My mom was always behind me limping along with her head down, concentrating on the ground so she wouldn't fall. Each step she took burned her already-sunburned legs. You wouldn't be able to tell that my mom was weak just by looking at her. Her calf muscles are bigger than most males'. She could probably even hold her own in an arm-wrestling competition. But the main thing that makes my mom strong is her eyes. I don't know if you have ever seen an eagle up close, but their eyes are penetrating, full of knowledge and pride. They seem to look right through you. If my mom were as strong as her eyes, they wouldn't have used an eagle for our national mascot. You would have found her on the back of the quarter instead. My mom's hair is already gray, so she would have blended in right under the words "E Pluribus Unum." The sad thing is, she isn't as strong as her eyes.

The problem was that in the years past she had five neck surgeries, so oftentimes she had to wear a neck brace. It made her look weak and helpless. To even see the ground, she had to bend over and walk much like a monkey with her arms dangling and waddling back and forth. Now imagine an excited boy running around and a mom who is in an awkward, bent-over position trying to keep up, and you could understand the majority of our Vegas vacation.

I remember looking back at my mom and seeing the pain in her face over and over again. But she always pushed on just to make me happy. I knew she was in pain every step that she took, but she is as stubborn as a mule. I would occasionally ask her if she would want to stop, but she would always say, "Do you want to?" followed by a few brief moments of silence.

"Not particularly."

"Then let's move on."

I knew she wanted to quit and just fall to the ground, but she didn't, and she tried her best to hide her pain from me. Eventually, I would stop and say I was tired just to give her a break.

"Can't keep up with an old woman, eh?" she would say, panting and trying to fake some kind of cheesy smile.

"I guess not," I returned with an overabundance of exaggeration. I laughed about it then, but a few moments later I watched my mom slip off the neck brace, stained by her own sweat, and limp over to buy a cold drink. I looked away half in humiliation and half out of pity as I thought to myself, "Why can't she be normal? No neck brace, no pain."

I remembered a time when I was younger when we could go to the park and play on the rusted slides. Or play baseball on the backyard lawn that she would help me mow week after week. She was my only friend in the entire world. But that time was gone, and years later there we were in Las Vegas trying to save an already-damaged relationship. You see, when I was around fourteen years old, my mother and I couldn't be in the same room with each other without arguing over things like what was for supper, or my math grades, or whose religious philosophy was better. There was constant bitterness between us in every conversation we had. Every day grew more intense, and finally, with one comment, I changed both our lives forever.

"I'm moving to Grandma's." The air became silent and almost cold.

"What?" my mom said, more shocked than angry.

"I hate you." The words came out of my mouth like bullets with one final destination. As I tromped off to my bedroom, I heard the sound of my mom whimpering as she sat down on the couch and dropped her face into her hands. In my head, I was happy. But my heart was still with my mom in the other room trying to take back the words I said that would cause years of silence between the two of us.

At that moment I knew my mom had more love for me than I could ever imagine, because as I left the house, she let me go.

After I left, my mom got sick. She had a disorder, Klippel-Feil syndrome, that caused her neck to have bone spurs, and every time it happened she had to have a surgery. I was always in school, and the surgeries were scattered from Phoenix to Boise, so I really didn't see her much. My grandma would always go with her and call to tell me how she was doing, but most of the time my mom couldn't talk because most of the surgeries were through her mouth.

When high school hit, I became involved in every club and every organization that was in our school. Time with family was scarce, and since I still lived with my grandparents, activities with my mom could be counted on fingers. So after watching my mom go through hospital bed after hospital bed, there we were in Sin City, sitting at a sidewalk café, talking like old friends who hadn't had a real conversation in a long time. It was nice; I found out that my mother is one of the funniest people I know. She is also very passionate about her beliefs, and when it came to our differences we just had to agree to disagree. The funniest thing was that I realized that despite our disagreements, we are more alike than anyone else I have ever met.

After our Vegas vacation was over, we went home closer than I ever thought we could be the day I moved out of her house. We still argue about what's for supper and why I won't get my math credit out of the way, but we understand each other better, and when we fight we work through the storm until we are both calm and clear. Now, every time I make the trip to Burley and pull into the front yard of her house, I knock on the front door and listen for the sound of approaching footsteps. As the door opens and I see my mom standing in the archway, and even though the sun doesn't reflect off her face, when I look at my mother, I see myself. My mother is beautiful.

/ / / / /

This story was written roughly fifteen years ago for a college English class that has long since been forgotten. I now see so clearly that I was unable to talk about the fact that my mom was a lesbian. I talked about her health, and our differences in opinion, and even moving out. But, due to the overwhelming shame and fear I felt about the situation, I couldn't muster the words to talk about it and how that had served as the main point of conflict that affected our relationship during my adolescence. I am so sorry that I never opened up. I wish I would have been like Tina's parents, who led with love, but I was just an angry child still struggling to understand why I didn't have a dad and my mom was a lesbian.

CHAPTER 3

Finding My Religion

MY GRANDPARENTS WERE LIFELONG MEMBERS OF The Church of Jesus Christ of Latter-day Saints. My mom was most definitely not. While I was baptized at eight—due largely to the fact that my mom and I spent weekends at my grandparents' and they were very persistent about it—I didn't have much to do with the Church for the years after that beyond the occasional sacrament meetings and random scouting campouts. Even those outings came to a fairly abrupt end when I got in a fistfight during a game of capture the flag. So moving in with my grandparents in the middle of junior high left me somewhere between the "Rock of our Redeemer" and a hard place when it came to church activities.

The years I had spent living with my moms led me to have a less-than-stellar view of "the Church" and "the Brethren," due to my mom sharing her stories of being an outsider growing up. She was scorned and hounded by leaders who didn't understand her and shunned by the youth her age that should have befriended her. Instead of positive experiences that those who are struggling desperately need, she left high school feeling like the only thing her church experience brought her was a heavy hand and pointing fingers. She didn't believe any of it. From her perspective, if the people we so mean and judgmental, how could the Church be so good? On top of that, her study of anti-Mormon literature later in her life verified everything about her experience in her mind, and she freely shared what she had learned with me.

I even remember getting into a heated argument with one of my friends about the Church's doctrine on the three degrees of glory in heaven. My friend told me about it, and I told him that he was crazy and that I would rather go to hell than believe such a thing! I told him that wasn't the teaching of the Bible and that he had better study harder. The irony is that doctrine actually was in the Bible—1 Corinthians 15, to be exact—but neither of us would have known that at fourteen. Ultimately, through most of junior high I wanted nothing to do with the Church. I didn't like it. I felt out of place being surrounded by a bunch of families that seemed to be so perfect from an outsider's view, while I felt like my family had more issues than a magazine stand.

Due to our discomfort with The Church of Jesus Christ of Latter-day Saints, my mom and I toured different churches in Burley with various friends and acquaintances over the years. One friend, John, took me to a lot of youth events at the United Methodist church in our town. The leaders and people were so nice and accepting of me instantly. I never felt judged, looked down on, or different. We even went to his church camp for a week, and I had what I would consider to be my first major spiritual experience where I gained a belief in Jesus Christ as I was sitting on a log deep in the mountains of Idaho while listening to a camp director tell stories about the Savior's life from the Bible. As he talked, I felt my heart beat through my chest, and his words sank into my soul. It was like pure knowledge that was opening my mind to a new world, to the possibility that there was a God and that He did have a son who was the Savior of the world. It was so simple, and I knew so little, but for the first time in my life I had a greater desire to learn at least a little more.

Even with the positive experience with my friend at his church camp, I still did my best to avoid going to church with my grandparents. I played the sick, tired, busy, and homework cards more times than I care to admit. One of my best tricks was to conveniently stay the night with friends on Saturday so I wouldn't be home on Sunday.

The thing I didn't account for was that some of my friends were Latter-day Saints—even if we argued about degrees of glory—and there was a string of Sunday missionary farewells happening when I was around fifteen that I got dragged to. A farewell was a special talk given by a young man or woman who was going to be leaving on a mission for the Church. Many of my friends' older brothers were going, and I figured if I had to go to church at least I could go with buddies and listen to their older brothers' talks. After all, these were the "cool" kids that I looked up to that did crazy stuff like build bike ramp jumps into the river, or climb two-hundred-foot radio towers on dates to win a kiss, or wakeboard in canals with a swimsuit being optional.

One experience in particular marked a turning point for me and my view of the Church. My friend Levi's older brother was leaving on a mission and gave an awesome talk in his congregation. Later that night he was getting set apart as a missionary before leaving for two years the next morning and had invited me to come over. Beforehand, he turned to all of us younger kids and told us how he knew what he was doing was right and that he had read the Book of Mormon and knew it was true. The words he said were simple and heartfelt, and I experienced again the same feeling that I had felt so long ago sitting on a log in the mountains with the Methodists. As he left for the Missionary Training Center in Utah and my friends and I drove home together along the snowy country roads, we were secretly wiping tears from our eyes while trying to ensure nobody else noticed. That is the only time I ever saw any of them cry. After that, I slowly began to think that maybe church on Sunday wasn't quite so bad if I could hear my friends talk.

As I put together my class schedule when I was a sophomore, I saw seminary, which was a released time from school to take a religion class, listed as an option and asked a friend what subject was being studied that year. I found out that it was the Old Testament. I figured it would be a safe way to get involved without being "too Mormony," so I signed up. I still had my suspicions, doubts, and doctrinal disagreements. I just simply couldn't deny that these boys I looked up to had a deep-rooted passion and belief in this religion that had been an unsolved mystery to me for years. I mean, they were willing to leave their friends and family for two years to go to a foreign land to share the gospel they believed to be true, and I just couldn't wrap my head around what it would take to believe in something enough to do that. I found it intriguing and unsettling enough that over time I began to really desire to find out for myself if I believed or not.

When it came time for college, I had narrowed the choices down to Utah State and BYU–Idaho. I wasn't a full-fledged believing Latter-day Saint by this time. More of a half-fledged one. But I had a lot of friends going to the school, and it was cheap, so I figured I would at least apply as a back-up plan to Utah State. I was accepted to Utah State with a very basic scholarship that would have still made it fairly expensive to attend. My application for BYU–Idaho, on the other hand, wasn't in by the deadline because the ecclesiastical endorsement didn't make it to admissions due to getting lost on the stake president's desk. So I was shocked when I got a denial letter, and I immediately talked to my bishop to find out what went wrong. Within a couple of days he got back to me and basically said, "Look, I can get you into the school, but if I do this you have to let me know right now that it is what you want, and you have to promise to go." I could have easily said no. I wasn't planning on going there in the first place. The fact that I had been denied just bugged me. I hated feeling like I couldn't.

I have no idea why, but I said yes. He made the call and got me in for the fall and winter track.

There are a few moments in life when we stand in front of doors that open to completely new worlds, and yet we think we are doing nothing more than making a choice to walk into another room. The decision to go to BYU–Idaho changed everything for me.

The week before I left for college I made a list of things I wanted to accomplish.

Write a song
Do improv comedy
Write a book
Paint a picture

It was a random list. I don't know why I wrote it, but one night I was in a contemplative goal-setting mode. You know, one that you find yourself in roughly once every few years or so, and I just thought through things that would make me feel like I accomplished something with my life. I didn't really have a timeline in mind. I just had these things I wanted to do and hoped that they would happen. There was no plan put into place. Just blind hope.

Instead of rooming with friends that first year, I decided it would be best to just take a gamble and move in with a bunch of random people. My first week at school I found out that two neighbors of mine were in a campus group called Comic Frenzy. The group just so happened to be an improv comedy club that put on shows throughout the semester to packed houses of students who didn't have anything else to do on Friday nights. I didn't even know the school had a club like that. I had never attempted improv comedy before but had been in quite a few comedies in high school plays and had stayed at a Holiday Inn once, so I figured I could give it a shot. I tried out and made the squad. I was the only pre-missionary freshman to do so and was affectionately given the nickname Mike "My Gramzy" Ramsey. If you say My Gramzy fast enough, it sounds like you are just saying my name. Only improv folks could find pleasure in that—and they did—and I got the nickname. One of my big life goals had been fulfilled practically by accident and through very little thought of my own.

Around that same time, I was sitting in the Galley (the cause of many students gaining the dreaded freshman fifteen) and happened to notice a curly-haired young woman walk by one day, and my exact train of thought went something like this:

"Wow, I have got to meet her."

"Yeah right, there is no way that is ever going to happen."

"She's walking away—you might not ever see her again!"

"Which will save you from the experience of ultimate rejection."

"You're probably right."

"Of course I am."

I figured I would never see her again. Then, at one of our improv comedy practices she walked into the room, smiled at me, and said her name was Tia and that she helped the club out.

I think I just stared at her and smiled back sheepishly in utter shock. Within a very short time, we became great friends. We would talk for hours, and I came to find out how spiritually strong of an individual she was. She also loved the arts with a deep passion and on Monday nights would have a group of friends over for an acoustic open-mic show. I was an avid fan of playing guitar but hadn't written much in the way of my own music. Through the experiences that I had with her over the coming months and the friendship we had, I wrote an entire album, headlined at a campus show, and sold around one hundred CDs for three whole dollars apiece. It was called The Bedroom Record (because I recorded everything in my college bedroom on an old mic hooked up to my computer). I didn't have editing equipment, so I just had to nail the song the whole way through for a good track, which took a very long time and probably dropped my grades down a little further than I should have allowed.

Tia was the perfect mentor to help me figure out who I was and what I was coming to believe about God, myself, and my purpose at that time.

The conversations I had with her caused me to reflect a ton on my life up to that point and how I was still torn between two worlds of thought. I couldn't say that I fully believed that The Church of Jesus Christ of Latter-day Saints was what it claimed to be. I didn't know where I stood on my relationship with my mom. I didn't know if I believed Joseph Smith's story. I didn't know if I believed the Book of Mormon was more than just a made-up manuscript, and I definitely wasn't sure if the Church was actually led by a real prophet.

I bought a journal and wrote, and wrote, and wrote. I covered my struggles, what was happening with school, ideas for songs and poems, and definitely my back-and-forth battle on what to believe. The writings filled up pages, and the pages became thick enough to be a book in no time, which led to me accidentally fulfilling another item from my list.

I decided the only way I was ever going to know for sure about this whole "Mormon thing" was to sit down and read the Book of Mormon from beginning to end for myself. I had never done it. Sure, I had heard stories and read things here and there. But I hadn't devoured it the way that I had the Harry Potter series, Jurassic Park, the Berenstain Bears (when I was younger), or a number of other books that I couldn't get enough of.

It took me a month to read the 527 pages of scripture.

Before starting, I couldn't even tell you what the Book of Mormon actually was or how it came to be. I thought it was just a bunch of things Joseph Smith must have written about God, much like a journal. I wasn't even close.

The quick explanation of The Book of Mormon is this:

At the age of fourteen, Joseph Smith said he saw God and Jesus Christ. Two separate people. He told many in his town, and they thought he was crazy. Some believed. Over the next several years, he had many angelic visitations and was led to an ancient record written on golden plates. He got the record when he was twenty-one, and then he translated it. The record is the Book of Mormon, and like the Bible, it gives a spiritual and historical account of a group of people. These people were from Jerusalem around 600 BC. They left the city and sailed across the ocean and landed in the Americas. The civilization grew. Part stayed true to the God of Israel, and part didn't. The Book of Mormon is basically a record of God's dealings with this people over 1,200 years.

As I read, I came to understand that either Joseph fabricated the story or it was actually a true record of a historic people. It was one or the other. True or false. If it was true, then the other events Joseph experienced must have been as well, and he was chosen by God. If it was false, then it would be the greatest hoax in American history and Joseph deserved an award for creating a two-hundred-plus-year hoax.

Those ideas went back and forth as I read the pages. True or false. Good or bad. I couldn't stop thinking about it. The more I read, the more I came to understand the lives of Nephi, King Benjamin, Abinadi, Alma, Ammon, and Captain Moroni, and the lessons I learned were so deep and strong that they touched my soul in a way that not many things had ever done before.

I remember weeping when Abinadi was tied up and burned at the stake for standing up to wicked priests and a king who were trying to justify and cover their sins. I could relate with Enos's mighty wrestle he had with God over the words that his father had taught him about the Savior's forgiveness of sins. I had that wrestle many times and was in the process of it while reading. I saw the faith of Nephi in going forward being led by the Holy Ghost, not knowing exactly what to do in very dangerous situations. All in all, each story came alive and sang to my soul.

During this process, I wrote a poem that summed up reading the Book of Mormon for me:

I read the pages of ages pass over my eyes
I watched civilizations nourished and flourish
But eventually fall and die.
It wasn't the great cities built and burned
It wasn't the long journeys where lessons were learned
It was me, and my Father, reading cover to cover
A book, a book about my Brother.

I went from believing I was a fatherless only child to believing that I had a loving Father in Heaven and a spiritual brother in His Son Jesus Christ in a deeper way than ever before. I understood more about them and how they worked with mankind, and I desired to know so much more.

When I finished the Book of Mormon, I went to the infamous Porter Park, sat at a base of an available tree—most of the trees were taken by young college lovers trying to blossom a romance, so it took time to find an open spot—and prayed.

It was the hardest and longest I had prayed up to that point in my life. I bore my soul to God and recounted every struggle, every triumph, every fear, every doubt, every loss, and every hope. Was Joseph Smith called of God? Was the Book of Mormon truly an ancient record? Does God speak to mankind through a prophet? Can I forgive myself and be forgiven for all my shortcomings?

It all came down to asking a single question.

"Is it true?"

As I asked the question and sat waiting for an answer, the silence that engulfed me was palpable. The giggles from tree-shaded couples subsided, and I sat in my own world of thoughts for what seemed like an eternity. Just as I was about to lose hope in receiving an answer to my prayer, I felt, not heard, the words come to my mind in a gentle but direct way:

"You have always known it's true; you just didn't want to admit it to yourself."

I instantly thought about all the times sitting in sacrament meetings I didn't want to be in, the times I did everything in my power to avoid going to "church things," the anger I felt toward those who had hurt my mom before, and I knew that the words felt in my mind were absolutely right. All the issues I had seemed to center around people, not the teachings. It didn't come across as a harsh reality—actually, just the opposite. But it cut me to my soul as if truer words had never been spoken to my heart. It was the first time I felt like I had truly received, and identified, revelation from God. He spoke to me, and I felt it. I liked it. It opened my mind and heart in a way I can't explain, and it left me wanting to continue to have experiences of enlightenment and revelation like that.

It took a lifetime of events and learning and being in the exact right places at the right times. But in that instant, I became a believing Latter-day Saint. That change and desire to continue to receive revelation from God would shape my life in ways I wouldn't comprehend fully for years.

With my newfound faith, I went to talk to the leader over my student congregation, Bishop Jack Weyland. I told him about my life that had been spent half in and half out of the gospel. I joked with him that he'd better not share my life events in one of his books, given that he was one of the more prolific Latter-day Saint romance and faith authors of the time and one of his books, *Charly*, had just been made into a movie. I guess with my writing this story instead, he will get the last laugh.

He recommended that I get a patriarchal blessing. I had no idea what that was, so he explained that it was a blessing given by a patriarch to Church members that can help individuals understand their life's mission, cautions, and blessings. I said okay, and he scheduled a meeting with Norman Nef, who was the patriarch over the college.

I have no idea how many students got patriarchal blessings at college. I imagine that most had their blessing before leaving home and am sure I was one of the few who slipped through the cracks and made it to college without one. It could easily be chalked up to my complete immaturity in the gospel when I was back in Burley, and I am extremely grateful that I was where I was when the time came.

I had never met Brother Nef before the blessing, and he knew extremely little about me. We spoke for a very brief time, and I was surprised that he didn't ask detailed questions. He asked why I wanted to get the blessing and where I came from. That was roughly the extent of our conversation.

Patriarchal blessings are very individual and sacred, so I will not go into depth about mine. I will simply share that I really wondered if I would ever go on a mission. I had mixed emotions about going and wasn't sure if I could, considering I hadn't even been fully active and "in the Church" until a few months before. I also was extremely worried about what my mom would think.

There was a pause as he was giving the blessing, and then he said, "It will be your privilege to be called to serve a mission." Tears immediately began to roll down my face, and I don't remember much of what was said for the next few minutes. I'm extremely grateful that the blessings are recorded and typed because I would have remembered only that line from mine.

As I left the building to go home, my head was spinning as those words repeated over in my mind. I was going to go on a mission. Every decision I made for the rest of that year in Rexburg was geared toward that. I made personal promises to read my scriptures, attend meetings, take a mission preparation class, and even to not kiss any more girls before I left to ensure maximum preparation. I completed three out of four of those goals and will let you be the judge on the one I didn't fulfill. Bottom line, I was determined and ready to take on the world.

On the last day of the semester, Tia called me to come visit her. As I made the familiar trip to her apartment, this time I reflected back on the year and how much had been accomplished and ultimately how much I had changed. When I walked in, she told me that she wanted to show me something and proceeded to hand me a beautiful painting of the Savior that she had just finished. This wasn't a normal picture though. She had painted the Savior as a puzzle being put together with the last piece about to be put into place.

As I stared at the painting, a flood of emotion hit me as I remembered the list of goals I made before the start of the year. I had created an entire CD, let alone a song. I acted in an improv group in front of hundreds of people. I even wrote a book of remembrance about the year. The only thing I hadn't done was paint a picture. It was fitting that instead of me painting it, the picture would be a gift. I saw my life up to that point represented perfectly in the frame: there were a bunch of puzzle pieces that I didn't understand, but over the past year things had fit together to reveal the Savior, who was there the whole time simply waiting for me to realize it.

The puzzle pieces in each of our lives are often not understood at the time they come to be. Individually, events and situations may seem meaningless, jagged, and even painful. Collectively, you begin to see how God works in our lives. I generally find the corner pieces are people, those mentors that come into our lives to show us a better way. It may be one person many times, or many people who are there at the right time. Each has something to share, or do, that lifts you a little higher. Then, you are on another plane and can be that mentor for another. I will be forever grateful to those people who came into my life and helped me find God and start learning how to communicate with Him. My mom taught me how to be spiritual, my friend John helped me to begin believing in Jesus, my grandparents and friends helped me get past hard feelings about the Church, and Tia helped me realize that I could find, seek, and know things that are true and eternal.

All of these people opened new worlds to me, and I was left with the epic goal of learning God's will for my life and set out on my new life of trying to follow His guidance. Seeking revelation became the very center of my life and purpose. I wanted to serve God, and I thought I was ready and willing to do just that.

There was one area in life where my newfound faith still didn't have all the answers for me yet. My mother was still a mystery to me. As I dove deeper into my faith, it was almost like I couldn't deal with my questions about homosexuality and avoided the subject entirely, due to being a little too afraid of what I would find, and I was not willing or ready to dive into the complexity of my feelings on the subject just yet.

My mom didn't talk much about religion with me after I moved in with my grandparents. I'm sure she understood how sensitive a subject it was, and she was careful to ensure that our little time together was positive. I knew it bothered her that I had embraced the church that had been a point of so much conflict and struggle in her life. I don't think she appreciated that I chose BYU–Idaho over her alma mater. Yet she still dropped me off at school and helped me get to know the campus. She came to a few of my performances. She let me find my own path, even if it was directly down a road that she feared the most—me serving a mission and becoming a full-on Latter-day Saint. Ultimately, I could sum up how my mom dealt with me moving out and embracing the Church with one word that would prove to be exactly what I would need to eventually understand her: patience.

CHAPTER 4

"Patience" Is a Four-Letter Word . . . So Is "Mission"

I DIDN'T KNOW ANYONE WHO WAS as excited to serve a mission as I was. The prophet Lehi, in the Book of Mormon, talked about having a vision in which he partook the fruit of the tree of life and immediately felt the desire to share it with others. I felt that same desire and wanted to proclaim it from the rooftops in a suit with a name badge as soon as I possibly could. With the semester ending and my birthday in June, I figured I would have my mission call within a few weeks and be in the mission field by mid-summer.

The paperwork was slow and arduous. My sudden change and my excitement to serve a mission baffled my bishop in Burley. After all, I had largely been inactive through my teenage years and showed no sign of wanting to serve. He wanted to ensure I was ready, so he decided to table my application for a while. The weeks that went by felt like I was running with a parachute on my back. I was angry and impatient, and it showed. I felt like I had a complete change of heart and couldn't imagine waiting any longer to get out and serve.

Finally, I scheduled a time to meet again with my bishop, and as we sat down I looked him in the eye and said that I was ready. He looked at me for a while, and with a smile on his face, he said, "Then let's proceed!"

After the paperwork was submitted, we all assumed that the mission call would come two weeks later on a Thursday. I have never counted minutes and hours and days so closely.

I wondered where I would go, and I secretly hoped to be in a foreign country speaking Spanish. I wondered if I would leave in the mid-summer like many of my other friends. I wondered if learning a language would be hard or if I would end up speaking English and serving in Wyoming or another place so close that on a clear day I could see it from the top of our local mountain. The questions circled in my mind with such intensity it was hard to eat, sleep, or focus on much else.

Finally, the appointed Thursday arrived! I ran to the mailbox so fast as the postman pulled away that the exhaust from his engine caused me to cough and rub my burning eyes as I tore through the newspapers and ads to find the envelope I had been waiting for.

My mission call wasn't there.

I slammed the box shut and checked the neighbors' mailboxes on either side just to ensure all the pieces made it in the right holes.

Still no luck.

I made my way back to the house in clear defeat with nothing to show for my quick effort other than a pile of crumbled junk mail that had faced my wrath and clothes that smelled like they had been on a mechanic fixing an exhaust pipe.

If the time I spent waiting was like running with a parachute attached before, then the time waiting for the next week to pass was like trying to run with no legs at all! I owe an apology to everyone who had the displeasure to cross my path during that week. Somehow, I made it through with minimal casualties. I went back to the same mailbox that had ruled my day seven days prior, knowing full well that surely this week would be different.

Nothing.

Then nothing the next week, or the next, and even the one after that.

For two and a half months I went to the mailbox to find nothing but disappointment, accumulating dents, and junk mail.

I had lost all faith and hope in going on a mission by this point and suspected that Lucifer, the slithery devil himself, had intercepted my missionary application and burned it in his smoldering eternal pit to ensure I never went at all. So much time passed that even my local bishop and stake president, who were the embodiment of patience due to years working with cows on a dairy, were sure that something was wrong. They called the Salt Lake City Church missionary offices and asked what was going on. The answer they got was that there simply wasn't a call issued yet and that I should be patient but trust that all was well.

This as least curbed my Lucifer theory, but not much else. I wondered why Heavenly Father would postpone me going on a mission when I wanted to go with every fiber of my being, and it was getting harder and harder to keep my excitement and the fiery darts of the adversary away. Two weeks later, on the day that I was leaving with a folk-dance group to Zacatecas, Mexico—that's a story for another day—my call came.

To avoid another confrontation with the mailbox, I asked the post office to hold all of the mail destined for our house to ensure that if the call came I could grab it before leaving in the minivan caravan headed for the airport. As I walked into the post office, Matt saw me from behind his counter and smiled, which instantly told me that my call was finally here. He handed me an envelope and said, "That looks like a good one. If it weren't a federal offense, I would have opened it myself!"

I thanked him and drove over to the gym, where we were having a quick practice before departing. Surrounded by family, friends, and dancers, I opened the envelope and read the words, "You will be called to labor for the period of two years in the England Birmingham Mission. You will speak the English language."

Everyone was so excited. Shouts to convert Harry Potter, James Bond, and the queen filled the air. In the midst of the fanfare, I noticed one person out of the corner of my eye that didn't seem as excited as everyone else. My mother. She was half-smiling. But I also noticed tears. It was the first time I realized how hard it was for her to support me down a path she didn't want me to take. She gave me a hug and congratulated me nonetheless, and I was quickly whisked away in a van headed for the airport and our festival. My mind moved on to the adventures ahead, but I'm sure hers focused on the inevitable day when I would leave and the day when I would come back a different person.

I had never in all of my wildest dreams imagined England as a place I might go on a mission. The second I heard it, I felt peace and comfort with a dash of calmness while everyone around me was clapping, laughing, and congratulating. Then, I read I would report to the mission field on October 20, which was another four months away, and all the peace, comfort, and calmness I felt before was replaced with the opposite attributes instantly.

If you haven't discovered yet that patience was, and continues to be, an attribute that I would need to work on, then let the rest of this chapter—and book, for that matter—be a testament to you of my greatest weakness. I've always wanted instant answers and understanding about the complexities of life. Why did I need to wait so long to get a call? Why did I have to wait so long to leave? Why was my mom gay? Ultimately, I have always wanted the knowledge that immediate answers provide more than the wisdom that comes from experience. The problem is that the most important answers in life can't be understood without wisdom. So maybe the answer and solution is patience.

/////

In late August of that year, I had the opportunity to go through the temple, as all future missionaries do before they leave. I had a group of friends from high school that were going to Utah a few days prior, and I figured I could go with them and meet my grandparents in Salt Lake City for my first temple session.

My friend group from Burley was very mixed. Half were really good, and even great, kids. They made choices that parents would be proud of (mostly) and were already out serving missions across the world. The great ones who weren't members of the Church were equally engaged in a good cause and diving far into programs in various university studies. The rest were all great and extremely fun guys, but a good way to put it would be to say that they were still trying to find their way through a desert of distractions and tended to stumble into epic experiences and challenges that would put the Las Vegas strip to shame. The latter friends were the group I was meeting in Utah.

The first night we stayed at a friend's house and went to what would be considered an average college party. I sat alone on the couch inside while my friends congregated in a circle in the backyard passing around a joint.

As I sat there, I contrasted my current situation with the uplifting experiences I had at college over the previous year. The difference was as noticeable as an electric guitar at a strings concert. I found that I had grown to like the sweet and simple life along with the rules that strings abide by compared to the hardpounding limitless decibels that my friends continued to flock to and seek more of. In the end, I didn't want to be there, and I got up and walked back to the apartment where we were staying. As I walked away from the party, each step felt lighter and my thoughts became clearer. I was at peace with myself and who I had become. I didn't need to rely on votes of confidence from my friends or new acquaintances because for the first time in my life I felt like the only people I had to impress were Heavenly Father and myself.

The next day my friends and I met up with some girls who lived in an apartment a few blocks from Temple Square. My friends had one thing on their minds that night, and it was not the square a few blocks away. As it got later and later, I felt more and more out of place, similar to the night before. I told the group I was going to go on a walk and ended up sitting on a bench staring at the well-lit temple. The hours went by as street cleaners and graveyard shift workers skirted across the square, but I sat unmoved until the dawn lights started to make their way over the Wasatch Mountain Front. Then I went back to the apartment while everyone was sleeping. I put on my church clothes and met my grandparents at the gate of the temple.

More than anything these experiences showed me the change I had gone through and the direction I wanted to point toward. I went into the temple feeling ready, honest with myself and with God, and excited. In exact opposition to the previous nights, I felt completely at home and was ready to hear the symphony of teachings that the temple offers. It did not disappoint.

/////

The night before I left on my mission, I was set apart. The stake president asked my mom to say the prayer beforehand, and she was so frustrated that she left the room in tears. I went after her and tried to calm her down. She told me she was afraid of me leaving and all the "Mormons" trying to get her to go back to church, and she didn't want to give in. Most everyone in the room thought she was just sad about my departure, but in those moments before I left, I saw the raw defiance and animosity my mom still had for the church I was about to dedicate the next two years of my life to.

She didn't say that prayer that night.

As the stake president put his hands on my head and set me apart from the world as a full-time missionary, I was so torn. On one hand, it was exactly what I wanted to do. On the other, I could see that my mom was visibly devastated from the process taking place. After being set apart, I had to be with another male companion who held the priesthood. While this is a rule that is mainly based on safety and protection, this meant I couldn't go with my mom anywhere alone that evening. I couldn't go visit her and Tina at their house a mile down the road. I needed my grandpa to be with me at all times. That bothered her. I would love to say that getting set apart was a spiritual experience. For me, it was the opposite. It was filled with contention. I walked on eggshells the whole night while hoping that everyone could leave the room without offending the others.

The next morning, when I left from the Twin Falls airport, I couldn't help but notice the stark difference between my grandparents and my moms. My grandparents were proud. My grandpa had a smile from ear to ear and just kept telling me how great he thought I would do and how much he loved me. My mom could hardly talk. It looked more like she was at my funeral than simply telling me goodbye for a season. She was in black and could hardly get a word out. I could sense her frustration and mixed emotions, and she finally mustered a mix of "Are you sure you want to go?" and "You'll do good." But I knew she fundamentally disagreed with the whole thing. I was about to go try to convert people to a church she hated. She feared that I would change into one of the judgmental men that had hurt her so much in her youth. In contrast, I was naive to all that was about to happen to me and just desperately wanted to get on the plane and out of the awkward situation.

When I arrived in England I was ready to hit the ground running. In the first interview I had with the leader over all the missionaries, President Munday, he looked at me with his bright smile and asked why I was there. Though I hadn't told many people about my childhood and family life, I immediately opened up to him and told him that my mom was gay and didn't want me on a mission, my dad wasn't in the picture, and I had read the Book of Mormon and believed that it was the word of God and that I was ready to go to work.

He told me that he thought I would do absolutely great and he was excited to see what the Lord had in store for me. I was a little surprised at how open I was with him, but you have to understand how charismatic and powerful President Munday was. He had told all the incoming missionaries his story. He was adopted by a humble Latter-day Saint family in England and had married his high school sweetheart. They started their marriage with absolutely nothing, and now he was a thirty-nine-year-old mission president—which was unheard of—and a multi-millionaire. I loved absolutely everything about him. As I watched him speak and lead in that first day, he became one of the few men to gain my trust, and I made my mind up that I was going to learn as much as I could from him.

It was customary for all new missionaries to go out the first night they are at the mission home and knock doors with a more senior missionary. President Munday assigned me out with Elder Kessler, and we knocked a street and he let me talk at every door. We handed out two copies of the Book of Mormon and even got into a flat where we had a very promising conversation about the gospel with a young mother. She loved what we had to share and promised to read the Book of Mormon.

I left that street thinking that I was going to baptize thousands. It seemed so easy, fun, and exciting! Elder Kessler seemed pleasantly surprised at how eager and able I was and impressed with the success we had.

I went to bed on fire that night. Visions of families flocking to hear what we had to say danced in my head like sugarplums at Christmastime.

The next morning, we sat in President Munday's office eagerly waiting to hear our location and companion assignments for the next six weeks. One by one, the twenty missionaries that were in my group were assigned. Then President Munday said, "Elder Ramsey, you will be serving with Elder Christensen and will whitewash Wolverhampton."

I came to find out that whitewashing meant going to an area that hadn't had previous missionaries serving for a time. It meant starting from scratch. At the time, I felt honored to do it and thought that I must have been very special to have that responsibility right out of the gate.

Then we got to Wolverhampton. Our apartment was in shambles, it was super cold and foggy, and instead of going out and teaching, we had to spend a few days getting acquainted with things like bus routes and the location of Church members and our chapel and buying groceries, supplies, and so on. It made the time go by deathly slow when I was so ready to proclaim the gospel.

Finally, the day came where the work began. We prayed to know where we should knock doors, and Elder Christensen let me choose the street. As we started knocking doors, we were met with utter disgust. People slammed doors in our faces, they swore at us, and one person even threatened our lives!

It was a stark contrast to the experience I had previously and was my first real taste of humble pie that would be served to me over and over for the coming two years.

Day after day, month after month, we tried to find people to teach, help, and share the gospel with. We were met with constant rejection. I hung on to hope that the young mother in Birmingham that I had talked to had taken our challenge to read the Book of Mormon. We had an upcoming meeting that the missionaries over that area would be at, and I was excited to ask them how everything was going with her. When I caught up to them and asked about it, they said that they had gone for a follow-up appointment, but there was a sack on the door with the book in it along with a note saying to never come back. My heart broke. All I wanted to do was teach, but it seemed there was no one to listen.

To make matters worse, the first letter I received from my mom in the mission field said she didn't agree with the Church or my choice to go on a mission. She said I would spend two years trying to convert others to the gospel when she knew that deep down the main person I wanted to convert was her—and she would not be converted. It was an impossibly hard letter to receive, given my circumstances.

My faith that led me to go on a mission had driven a massive wedge even deeper between my mom and me. I know she did her best to support me as I told her I wanted to go on a mission, but she never could hide the fact that it was like losing me all over again. Now that I was gone, she really let her unbridled opinion be known. I truly feel for parents who aren't members of the Church and have to send a child off to the mission field. It's hard enough for those that are full-fledged believing members of the Church, but imagine watching your child say goodbye for two years so that they can learn and teach something that you openly oppose. In my mom's mind, I was on a path that would "indoctrinate" me to hate her because she was a lesbian.

It was a hard situation, and being across the world made communication tricky. I didn't know how much to share or write in fear of saying the wrong thing and offending her. I didn't want to be overly focused on religion in my letters to my mom, in order to avoid doctrinal arguments, and I also didn't want to talk about any of the hard stuff happening, for fear that she would look at it as godly punishment for choosing to serve a mission. It was confusing to think through as I was trying to find my place on the other side of the world.

Each day got colder and colder, along with my attitude. It culminated on December 22, 2013. I had been on my mission for three months and was battling a mixture of rain and snow while we waited at the bus stop to go to downtown Wolverhampton. When we got on the bus, I noticed this young family with a daughter that looked so bright and cheery. I had seen so few young families that actually had both parents in the picture, and I couldn't help but just watch as they played with their daughter. I decided that I had to talk to them and that this was going to be a happy turning point on my mission. Given that it was Christmastime, we were carrying Nativity DVDs, and I simply looked at the father and asked if he would like a free DVD about Jesus's birth for the Christmas season.

While I wish I could tell you that he accepted the gift with grace, he glared at me, pushed the DVD away, and said, "We aren't having this conversation, mate. Get out of here." I looked at him, said, "Merry Christmas," and walked back to my seat as my eyes started to water up. As I sat there, I had no idea why I was in England wasting my time. It had seemed as if I had zero effect, success, or positive stories to share about my experience to that point. As I thought about it, I became more and more upset and finally shouted loud enough for everyone on the bus to hear, "I hate this country!"

At that moment, I did. I couldn't think of anything redeemable in the people we had met and the places I had been over the previous months. As the day went on, I turned my thoughts toward the heavens and pleaded with Heavenly Father to help me understand what needed to change. I wanted success immediately and was willing to pay whatever price necessary to achieve that. I finally figured it out. The thing that needed to change was me.

I thought my abilities, my work ethic, my past, and my desire would be enough to make me successful as a missionary. What I realized was that I hadn't put my trust in God and had relied completely on my own strength. I had complained about how long it took to get my call and leave for the mission field instead of trusting that God knew the timeline, leaders, and places I needed to be. I had desired success as a missionary for my own pride, compared to truly loving the people I was serving regardless of how they reacted.

The answer from God, the revelation I so desperately sought, was to be patient. To keep knocking, keep asking, keep trying, and most important, keep loving. I needed to do everything in my power to serve and trust that Heavenly Father would put the right people in the right path at the right time and then put the right words in my mind to be a free-flowing instrument in His hands.

Two more months went by before we started to teach a family about the gospel of Jesus Christ and the Book of Mormon. When the time came, it was very little of what we did and so much more Heavenly Father bringing a person at the right time to the table. We had talked with hundreds and received various forms of rejection, but this family was the first to actually read the Book of Mormon for themselves, gain a belief, and put the gospel principles to practice. I witnessed a light come into their home that had previously been surrounded in darkness, and I pleaded with Heavenly Father daily that He would guide my words and actions to help them any way we could. He did.

Instead of pushing the family to all accept at once, we recognized that they each had an individual path that they needed to take. That was something I would have never accepted before my humbling experience. While it took months to see the full family join the Church, they all did it in their own time with God's help. To this day the memories I have in their home are some of the dearest memories of my entire life. I love them like my own family, and my heart breaks for their struggles and leaps for joy for their triumphs. They taught me what it meant to love the English.

I could write a whole book on lessons I learned in the mission field, and someday I will. By far the most important lesson I learned was that patience is a four-letter word.

It's love.

When you love God, you are willing to trust in His timing and endure with faith whatever afflictions you have to bear. When you love others, you are patient with their shortcomings and struggles and look at them through the Savior's eyes. When you develop this love for God and others, then you will find that ultimately you have love, which is patience, for yourself.

CHAPTER 5

Love . . . and More Patience

THE IDEA OF HAVING A STEADY girlfriend was hard for me through high school. My mom and Tina had tried to keep their relationship secretive, and that rubbed off on how I dated. I never talked to family, or even friends, about who I was interested in and rarely brought a girl around the house. I also avoided long-term relationships like the plague. That would have been far too public for my liking. It would have also forced me to open up about my feelings and home life, which was the last thing I wanted to do or talk about. There were very few girls who knew about my circumstances, and I was super fearful that the truth would halt any real relationship in its tracks. So I just did my best to keep the information at a distance. There was one exception to my secrecy game plan. Her name was Hillary.

We met in Burley on our school ski trip when I was fourteen. She was a year younger than me and had the biggest smile and bubbliest personality in at least a three-county area. We sat by each other on a bus ride home, and I asked her if she wanted to listen to a CD and proceeded to play the newly released Korn album on my super-groovy portable CD player. If you don't know who Korn is, that is probably a good thing.

Hillary had no idea, and I could see by the look on her face that she really wasn't liking the heavy metal guitar playing and all the swearing. So I told her I would hit the CD player to make it skip at just the right spots. She laughed and said okay. That was the start of her lifting me a little higher a step at a time.

As the years went on, I thought of her a bit differently compared to the other girls in high school. She always seemed to have a boyfriend, but deep down I think she always liked me while I played hard to get the whole time. Given that I am writing the book, that is the version of history that will hopefully be remembered, but if you ask her, our roles might have been reversed.

One of the good friends, and great examples, I mentioned that dragged me around to farewells throughout high school was Hillary's older brother Lucas. I spent a lot of time at their house and really loved all six of the kids and the parents. Lucas claims to this day that I just used him to be around his sister. Truthfully, I was drawn to the whole family. They were a loving, fun, welcoming bunch whose home functioned more like a hotel and café for teens than a traditional house. On any given day you could walk through the door, without knocking, and find one of your friends sitting at the kitchen counter eating a bowl of healthy cereal while the Handy family was nowhere to be found!

The Handys loved being members of The Church of Jesus Christ of Latter-day Saints. They loved God. A lot of it had to do with an accident that happened shortly after I had met Hillary. Each family member was a different character in the musical *Fiddler on the Roof,* which had just opened at the Oakley Howell

Opera Playhouse, twenty minutes from our town. They had loaded up a suburban with over ten people and were driving on the highway to make the casting call when they lost control of the vehicle and rolled countless times.

Not one of them had their seatbelt on, and only one person stayed in the car as it turned over and over. The rest were thrown out through broken windows and doors. Witnesses said they just saw more and more bodies flying out of the vehicle as it rolled into a farmer's field, and they figured there were multiple fatalities.

Miraculously, everyone lived. There were broken bones, and many of the group wound up in intensive care, but they all survived and have thrived ever since. If you talk to anyone involved in the accident, they claim that angels attended to them. The accident drew the family close together in ways that I don't think I can fully comprehend. They witnessed the fragility of life and felt they were saved for a purpose and have spent their time since in service to all around. Collectively, they are some of the most Christlike people I have ever met.

Hillary broke her lower back in the accident and had to spend over six weeks in a wheelchair. Luckily, no permanent damage was done, and before long she was back to dancing . . . and driving boys crazy.

She always used to look at me and say, "I love you . . . like a brother." It quickly led to me joining the ranks of said boys that had been driven down the crazy road by her antics. As a way to get back at her, I wrote a humorous song about the situation for a high school talent show. It was set to an old-time do-wop beat and is worth sharing the lyrics here even though you can't experience the full majestically sung version that won the Mr. BHS competition in 2002. The stage was dark, and I came out in a black '50s costume with a purple electric Fender guitar.

(Introduction set to a flowing strum)

Have you ever met the perfect girl and you just knew that she's the one? And one night you're going to tell her. You look up into her eyes, but before you can say anything she says this:

(Singing in a girl's soft and soothing voice)

"I love you with all my heart,
And I miss you when we are apart.
And I will never, ever find another . . .
Gee, I love you . . . like . . . a brother!"

(Back to dialogue and flowing strum)

A brother? Brothers and sisters don't even get along! They hate each other! Gosh, this always happens. You meet the perfect girl, and they're like, "We're too good of friends to be together." Why do you think they call them boy-FRIENDS and girl-FRIENDS? So I looked into her baby blue eyes and said this:

(Sung in a manly voice with a hint of disdain)

"How can you love me like a brother
When we didn't come from the same . . . mother?"

(Back to a girl's voice)

"But I can count on you when tears roll down my eyes,
And I can count on you when I have problems . . . with other guys."

(Dialogue with a little more disdain)

Yeah, that's right, other than "me" guys. That's when I got a little angry and said this:

(At this point I stepped on my pedal to turn the nice soft and smooth guitar into a static-filled electric-rock bringer of pain)

"I would rather pee on an electric fence,
Or get my head bashed in with a hammer till there's dents,
Or get hit with a frying pan by your mother
Than for you to ever say . . . you love me like a brother.
How could you ever be so cruel?
You tore my heart open and ripped it in two.
Well, I never really liked you, and I really hate your mother
(Just kidding—it's all that rhymes),
And as far as I'm concerned, you can never, ever, ever
Call me your brother!"

(Peaceful dialogue and back to the soft acoustic sound)

With that she slapped me in the face—ouch—and told me
that we could never be together. Now I know I didn't mean
those things I said to that little lady. And as I thought of a
way that we could be together, I remembered . . . brothers
and sisters could get married . . . in Arkansas!
So I looked at her and said . . .

(Sung in a loving manly voice)

"Let's move to a land where we're free,
Where brothers and sisters can get married,
'Cause you and I know it would be the best,
What we call love, others . . . would call incest."
(Loads of laughter and gasps from the audience)
"I love you with all my heart,
And I miss you when we are apart.
I will never, ever find another, so I guess it's okay
If you love me like a brother."

Hillary's friends looked at her halfway through and said that the song was "totally" about her. Of course, Hillary denied knowing anything. I cut my losses and went to Rexburg after my senior year with little hope that anything would ever happen.

When I came back from college a year and a half later, I wanted her to be my last date before I left on my mission. She had actually been my first date, so I figured it was only fitting. I wrote a letter telling her exactly how I felt about her, and I had it burning a hole in my pocket while I waited for the perfect opportunity to give it to her. As we sat and talked on a hill overlooking Burley, I simply couldn't muster the courage. It just didn't feel like the right time.

I wrote her a letter from the Missionary Training Center in Chorley, England. Then another in Wolverhampton and again in Derby. The letters went unanswered for months.

There is a perception on your mission that you can and should completely drop all thoughts of any "special someone" and focus 110 percent on the work at hand. I think this is partway true for most. I didn't spend days upon days thinking about Hillary while I was serving, and I never felt like she was a distraction. I was caught up in the things happening in England, and I learned to love it. That being said, there would be the occasional evening when the work was done and lights were about to go out and I would wonder where she was and what she was doing. She was one of the few that I felt like really knew me, after all. She knew my family, she knew my friends, and it never seemed to faze her. I appreciated that, and it put her at the top of my list for potential prospects after my mission.

December 9, 2014, was one of those nights. I couldn't get Hillary out of my mind. I wondered why I hadn't heard from her. I figured that there was no hope and that she was probably on the verge of marriage with some lucky bloke while I was an ocean away. So I sat down, and I wrote in my journal:

Letters Are Lost

Somewhere between here and your heart my letter was lost.
It must have been caught in the customs of courtship
that a man hasn't experienced because of fear.
But something says the letter was worth it,
The return, unexpected, but invitation open.
This is too deep for an envelope to understand, so I end it with
a letter:

I hope to hear from you soon. I wish my love was known, but the fear of rejection keeps me silent. Only a pen and a pad that you will never see, never know, and never want, will cry a love story to you, about a boy who met a girl and never had her. And about a girl who was a letter away, but the letters were lost.

Other than winning an award for the most melodramatic thing ever written, I decided that night that I was done. I wouldn't write her ever again, and I would move on. After all, there were plenty of fish in the sea, and I considered myself an excellent fisherman.

I went to bed with a firm resolve. The next morning, our doorbell rang, and as I opened the door the postman said, "I have a package from Hillary Handy for an Elder Ramsey."

It's a good thing that I had gone to the bathroom earlier, because if I hadn't I might have had an accident in my pants. I took the package and ripped it open like a little boy hoping for a Red Ryder BB gun on Christmas Day. There were pictures, candies, a tie, and a gift revered by missionaries since the dawn of the recorder: a talk tape.

A talk tape was basically a recorded cassette tape that functioned much like an instant messaging service before phones had the internet. People would record friends, events, and activities and then send it to a missionary to give them a little piece of home. Hillary's did not disappoint. She had recorded my friend's mission homecoming talk, some songs her family had sung, and lots of little messages from her about how she was doing and what was going on in her life. It was the ultimate sign that not only was she done ignoring my letters but that she was potentially nibbling on this fisherman's hook.

Some might say the timing of the package was a coincidence. After all, it could have been pure dumb luck after fifteen months in England that my thoughts would turn to Hillary with such force as to write a poem and resolve to be done only to receive a package from her the next day. My opinion is that the timing came from God. It was a tender mercy telling me to keep serving, be patient, don't forget about her, and trust that everything was in His hands.

I know I'm not the only one to experience situations like this. Time and time again you hear that someone is at the end of their rope. They can't bear to take one more step forward, and then someone steps in to lend a helping hand at a failing hour. Or a spiritual experience manifests itself and gives an added measure of strength.

I have tried to keep a record of these types of events in my own life so that when my faith dwindles due to whatever hard circumstance I find myself in, I can always remember.

I would have to draw on that remembrance much sooner than I thought.

With only a couple of weeks left in the mission field, I got a message from Hillary asking me on a date. Yet again, she might remember it differently, but *she* invited *me* to go with her and her family (which in her mind means it wasn't a date) to a dinner show the first weekend I was home.

I vividly remember the first time I saw her after my return. My friends were meeting at the tennis courts. I was excited to see them, but it was nothing compared to the anticipation I felt of seeing her. She got out of the car and yelled my name and ran across the courts and gave me the biggest hug I have ever had in my life. I felt like my heart literally stopped. For good measure and to keep things interesting, she said, "Welcome home . . . brother!"

We started dating immediately. It was the best time of my life, and I felt like everything was coming together. She was in the middle of a semester at BYU–Idaho, and I was washing windows for side money in Burley. It allowed me to set my own schedule, which meant that I spent a lot of nights on friends' couches in Rexburg and every waking moment of the day with Hillary. She was so beautiful, fun, spiritual, and happy. After seven years of knowing her, I truly was ready to spend the rest of my life with her.

There was one problem, though. Right before I got home from my mission, she had just gotten her own mission call to Arequipa, Peru, and was leaving in late December. Dating her at that time was like speeding up to a stoplight. Each day I fell more and more in love, but I knew that no matter how much we cared for each other, she was still going to go.

The day she left I drove back up to the hill overlooking Burley where we had sat together before I left on my mission. I prayed for patience.

Patience. Patience . . . Patience! That word has been one that has tried me to my wits' end more times than I care to admit. It seems like each time the test and length of the trial is pushed a little harder and further.

That year and a half was hard. I pushed myself to take twenty-plus credits a semester. I worked as hard as I could in the summer, and I compared every girl I met to Hillary, which made for many first and last dates—and many frustrated women.

Halfway through the waiting game, there arose a complication. Hillary had a boyfriend throughout high school. He had gone on a mission and was far out of sight and out of mind when we dated, due to him being a year younger than me and halfway across the world. Hillary told me that she had written him before she left and let him know we were dating, and I thought that had ended things with him. He was home now, and on one very unfortunate night at the Cassia County Fair and Rodeo (I'm not making this stuff up) I found out *from him* that she still had feelings for him and was writing to both of us.

As he told me the story of her letters to him, I felt physically sick. We both felt played and promised each other we would let her have it. I went home and wrote a harsh but truthful letter about how I wasn't willing to play any games or compete for her when she got back. I resolved that I was done, yet again, and tried my best to move on with my life.

I threw myself into school, work, and dating others and did my best to forget about Hillary. Months went by, but no matter how hard I tried, I couldn't stop thinking about her and realized that I was fishing, but simply playing the game of "catch and release" because there was only one keeper in my eyes. Okay, no more cheesy analogies.

Finally, around Christmastime, and after about six months of no communication between us, I sent her a package of things that I had gotten her during the summer. I was sure to say that I had been sitting on the gifts for a while, and I also threw in the fact that I had a "super serious girlfriend . . . and things were getting really serious. Seriously," for good measure in order to make sure she didn't read too far into it. But it rekindled the conversation through letters between us even though we proceeded with much more caution this time around.

As the letters progressed in frequency and thought, I realized that she would be home soon and that I needed to be in Burley when she was back. So I made arrangements to take time off of my summer door-to-door sales job in Utah and I got home a couple of days before she arrived. The anticipation was brutal. Yet again it seemed like time stood still, and I could count every heartbeat that passed as I waited for her to get back to Burley.

On the morning she arrived, it was if all the anticipation that had been building up was replaced in a single instant with a deep level of fear and trepidation, and I couldn't bring myself to go over and see her. I woke up, ate breakfast, and paced the house as the hours ticked by and I ran every scenario of how things could go through my mind like a choose-your-own-adventure movie. I now am fairly certain the fear was a godsend, due to the fact that if I would have gone over first thing, I would have landed at her door the same time her old boyfriend did, which would have made for an especially awkward homecoming surprise for us all.

By the early afternoon, I mustered up the courage to make the trek and went and visited her. It was awkward. Like walking-in-your-underwear-through-high-school-halls awkward. Her previous boyfriend had left only a few minutes before, and she was clearly agitated about the situation, so the visit was short and uneventful. The conversations were filled with small talk when we both had way more to say than either of us could find the words to utter. I didn't know exactly what to think about it, so I spent the remaining part of the day analyzing every word and movement, trying to find hidden signs that would help me decipher the sticky situation.

Later that day, I ended up meeting one of Hillary's older brothers (my former college roommate), Lucas, and he mentioned that he was planning on throwing a homecoming party for Hillary that night. He spent a good part of a half an hour trying to convince me that I should come despite the awkward encounter earlier in the day. I begrudgingly accepted and figured that a second visit couldn't possibly be worse than the first.

I have never been so wrong in my entire life.

That night as I walked through the door at the Handys', I couldn't help but notice that everyone's eyes darted back and forth between me and the formal living room where Hillary was in conversation with her old boyfriend again. In true Lucas fashion, he had invited us both, and I am pretty sure that the vast majority of the people in attendance showed up for two reasons. Lucas told them they could (1) eat free food, and (2) find out how the love triangle would play out.

The sight of her in conversation with the previous boyfriend left me feeling like someone was pushing a thousand needles into my chest a second at a time. Each second's prick added up until I literally felt sick, so I left before I even had a chance to say a word to her. I went home and sat in my own defeat and misery. By all accounts, I figured I had lost her before I even had the chance to really talk.

That night I poured my heart out in deep soul-searching prayer and wrestled with God. I had only one desire at that time of my life, and that was to be with her, but everything that happened over the past twenty-four hours had thrown the future I had been working on for the previous five years up in the air like ash from a destructive volcano covering everything I found to be beautiful in this life. I came to realize I needed to be okay with whatever the outcome may be. I asked for strength to move on if needed and for hope to realize that if Hillary was not meant to be in my life, then I could find the one who would be . . . someday.

Somewhere in the midst of my pleas I drifted off to sleep.

I don't remember many dreams. Usually when I do, they are crazy ones, like falling off buildings or running from people with guns. I rarely take them as meaningful experiences and chalk it up to an overactive imagination. But that night I had a very vivid and memorable dream. Hillary walked up to me with a smile and simply told me that she chose me. It was so simple and powerful that I woke up and knew instantly in my heart that it wasn't wishful thinking but something more.

I made the drive to the Idaho Falls temple that day, and as I sat in the celestial room I ran over the events that had occurred since Hillary came home and felt an overwhelming peace that the dream came from God.

When I got home, I was trying to decide if I should stay in Burley for a few more days to see how things would play out or head back to Utah and put in a few more days of work. As I was thinking through the choices, I walked outside and sat on the grass. As I looked up into the clear July sky, I saw two birds flying sporadically from tree branch to tree branch. As one would get close to the other, the first would dart away to a new location. This pattern went on and on. One bird chasing, the other running.

As I watched the chase with these birds unfold, a simple thought entered my mind. *If you keep chasing her, she will always run.* Then, as if the pursuing bird heard the same words in his own mind, he stopped, flew to his own branch, and waited. Within a minute the other bird flew and landed on the same branch where her pursuer stood his ground.

I left for Utah without seeing Hillary. It was hard. It was against my nature. But the message I received from watching two little birds in my yard was too direct to ignore. While the events of the previous few days—and years, for that matter—had tested me more than I care to admit, I can't recall a time I felt closer to the heavens. I had no doubt that my Heavenly Father was very aware of me, my desires, and my constant need for answers.

A week went by, and as it did, it became harder and harder to remember the sweet experiences that had given me the much-needed hope to make my way back to Utah. I was working as a door-to-door salesman, which was mentally grueling enough, and I found it virtually impossible to focus when my mind would wander to thoughts of Hillary between every door. If I saw a bird, I would think of her. If I saw a temple, I would recall my revelatory experiences of the week before. Given that I was in Utah, there was a plethora of birds and temples, so I didn't find a peaceful moment in my mind for days!

After the very long week, I decided I would make the trip home again. I wasn't sure if I would contact Hillary or not, but I had a feeling that I needed to at least be in Burley in case an opportunity presented itself. Also, I was plumb out of clean clothes and nobody could quite make my laundry smell as good as my grandma could, so I figured I had nothing to lose. I loaded up, put on my best iTunes mix, and ventured on the three-hour trek that would hopefully prove to be a better experience than the week prior.

The second I turned into my driveway in Burley, my phone rang. I looked down, almost had a heart attack, and quickly threw the car into park before it shot through the garage door.

It was Hillary's number.

A thousand words and emotions went off in my head all at once like the fireworks finale that I had witnessed just days before on the Fourth of July. I instantly thought of a hundred different things I wanted to say, from "It's so great to hear from you!" to

"What in the world took you a full week to reach out to me?" But in the end, the last thing I thought of before I answered was those two birds, and my nerves cooled.

"Hello?" After everything, that was literally the best I could come up with.

"Mike! Where have you been, mister, and why haven't you called?"

I literally couldn't believe the words I was hearing. All the apprehension that Hillary had shown in our first meeting melted away in two seconds on the phone call. She was the warm, bubbly girl I remembered. I could sense her nervousness by the giggles she let out after the slight rebuke but could also tell that she delivered the whole rehearsed line with a slight grin across her face.

"Well, uhh . . . I had to go back to work, and I figured you wanted some time with . . . your family," I said, cool like John Travolta in *Grease*.

I definitely wasn't going to tell her the whole story right then. I mean, what would you do if someone said, "Well, I had this dream, and then I went to the temple, and then these birds told me to go to Utah!"?

"I missed you! I haven't gotten a chance to show you pictures of my mission. Do you want to come over tonight, if you're not busy?"

Funny enough, Hillary made the first move to ask me on a date when I got home from my mission, and it looked like not much was changing this time around.

"Hillary, are you asking me on a date?" Sticking with the Travolta approach.

"I guess I am. See you soon."

As I put down the phone, I felt pure, unfiltered joy for the first time in years. Even before Hillary had left on her mission, it was like there was always a little shadow over the sun that constantly reminded me that she was bound to be off on her own adventures and I wouldn't be part of that. I was happy, but I always felt incomplete.

A brief phone conversation with her was enough for that shadow to start to disappear, and the sun came shining through.

/////

When I walked through the door at the Handys' house, I wasn't greeted with the awkward hug that I was met with a week before. This time around, she ran up to me and threw her arms around me with a squeeze that would have made a boa constrictor jealous.

We sat and talked for hours. She showed me pictures of the people who became her second family over the year and a half in Peru. She told me stories of her struggles to learn Spanish and her newfound love of spicy food and colorful clothing. The conversation flowed like we hadn't missed a beat. If I hadn't been sitting in the middle of it and an observer told me that this was the same girl that could hardly look me in the eyes a week ago, I would have told them that they were off their rocker.

At some point, our conversation found its way to talking about "us." I kept getting this nagging feeling that I should tell her about my dream. Then the logical part of my brain would kick in, and I would try to push the thought away so I wouldn't come off like a crazy person. The feeling kept coming back, so finally I told her that I had a dream in which she told me she had feelings for me.

She sat silent for a minute, and I figured I had completely blown it. To my surprise, she said that she had been going on dates with the other guy all week long but couldn't get her mind off me and spent the whole time wondering where I had disappeared to.

She grabbed my hand and pulled me in for an embrace that seemed to last an eternity. Even an eternity was still too short. I had spent so many years head over heels for this woman, and finally, after seven years, two countries, countless letters, heartbreak, hopes, fears, and tears, I knew she felt the same. Completely.

As I left the house I started driving and didn't really care where I went. I was in love and was loved in return, and nothing else mattered. Before long I realized that I was back to the hill that overlooked Burley. The same hill that I took her to before I left for my mission and where I went when she left. So much had happened. My dreams were coming true, and all I could do was give thanks to God. He gave me the patience needed to exercise faith in His plan for me. On my own I think I would have ruined my chances in a hundred different ways. Luckily, I was not alone. I had a Father who was watching out for me, one who knew my desires, struggles, shortcomings, and fears of finding a woman who could take me for who I was and the past that I had come from.

I later found out that while I had driven up to the butte overlooking Burley, Hillary had rushed into her parents' room (it was 2:00 a.m. by the time I left her house) and woke her parents up to tell them that she knew it was me. Her mind was made up.

The next few days went by in a blur. We spent every waking moment together. Each day I knew more and more that I wanted to spend "the forevers" with Hillary, and it became very apparent that she felt the same. One day when I was at home, I had the strongest feeling that I needed to pray, so I did.

I went to my room and got on my knees and just poured out my heart and soul in gratitude for how things were going. As I knelt there by my bed, words came to my mind. It wasn't a voice, more like sentences I could read and feel that said to me I had been faithful through my trials and trusted in God. It was time that I asked Hillary to marry me before school started back up in six weeks. I was also told not to tell anyone just yet and that as Hillary went to the temple that day with her family she would have the same feeling, and I would know when the time would be right to talk with her.

We were married on September 6, 2007, before the semester started. Hillary did have an experience, she said yes, and her poor mom had five and a half weeks to put together a wedding and a reception. Everything about the day was magical. We were surrounded by the people we loved, and the Idaho Falls temple sealing room was bursting over capacity.

As I looked around the sealing room, I saw my grandparents, Hillary's parents and older brothers and sister, and our friends. There were two people missing, though, that I wanted in that room so badly: my mom and Tina. Given that they weren't active Latter-day Saints with temple recommends, they weren't able to come inside. Instead, they were waiting outside with some of the younger kids.

I've never had the courage to ask my mom what she thought about that day. I know she looked happy for us when we walked out of the temple hand in hand, but I couldn't help but think of how hard it must have been for her to not witness the marriage of her only child. I wanted her in that room. I wanted Tina in the room. But I knew at that time it wasn't possible.

In England, it was customary for members of the Church to get "civilly" married in the morning and then get sealed that same day, due to the laws of the land. The same rule holds true for New Zealand. I liked that. It allowed for a level of inclusion for those who couldn't be in the temple, while still honoring the importance and significance of starting with a temple marriage.

I can't tell you how excited I was when the policy change in May 2019 was announced that gave Church members an option to have a civil marriage without waiting a year for a temple sealing. I would have loved to have been able to do that and have my moms at a civil wedding followed by a temple sealing. Weddings are not only a commitment between two people but a celebration of the union to be shared with family and friends, and many people who were very important to me weren't able to attend.

Any level of exclusion that my mom and Tina felt during our scaling was swallowed away by the level of love that Hillary showed them. From the time we first dated to this day, Hillary never let the fact that she was a Latter-day Saint and they were lesbians have any effect on the way she treated them, talked with them, or acted around them. I wish that all could say the same, but I have no doubt not only that some would feel uncomfortable with lesbians for mothers-in-law but also that it would have been enough to scratch me off the potential husband list from the beginning. My moms have always loved Hillary. I know they were extremely worried about who I would marry. There was a fear that if my spouse had a high level of discomfort with my moms that they would be written out of our lives and the lives of our children. So, without really talking to me about it, they were very hopeful that I would marry her because they knew they would have nothing to fear. Though they weren't in the temple during our sealing, they were able to attend the reception. We decided to forgo the normal Wasatch Front reception line, where both families line up on either side of the bride and groom in the church gym with tinsel hanging from the basketball hoops. Could you imagine trying to explain my familial relations to countless people walking through a line?

"This is my mom, and this is my other mom."

"Oh, so you have two dads. Where are they?"

"That's a great question. I mainly have two moms and no dads around."

"Oh. *Ohhhhh!*"

My mom and Tina would have died. It would have been like making them wear rainbow jumpsuits with signs pointing at them saying, "Get your chance to share pleasantries with two lesbians! Please don't make this awkward!"

Instead, we had a dance, and Hillary and I walked around and talked to those in attendance without the need to lay out genealogy for all in attendance. It was beautiful. My bride was beautiful. My moms had a great time, and I guarantee it was a better way of doing a reception than the never-ending awkward line that we have grown accustomed to.

As I look back on my love story with Hillary now, I see that it's a story of patience. I had to learn to wait, love, and trust in Heavenly Father's timing. Hillary grew so much on her mission that I couldn't have imagined her not having that time for herself to learn and grow, even if it was a brutal year and a half for me. Hillary had to learn to be patient with me as I grew from the boy who made her listen to Korn into a man that was constantly working on becoming better. She also was very patient with my kin as she realized that she would never have the big "Mormon in-law" family that young women are somewhat taught to idealize. I can't tell you how many times I have heard people say, "Well, I don't know much about so-and-so's fiancé, but they sure do come from a great Latter-day Saint family. I'm sure they will be just fine."

Instead, she had to have people ask her hard questions, and she had to defend against those who told her she was taking too big of a risk. She never once has complained or asked for my family to be anything more than who we are. More often than not, she invites my moms to be with her family for holidays and Sunday dinners.

Lastly, my mom had to have patience with me and my decision to marry in the temple. I know it wasn't easy for her to see me take that path, but she was supportive of the woman I chose, and I have never heard her complain to this day about it. I have no doubt they would choose Hillary over me any day!

Love is an exercise of patience. And, gratefully, my story has enough love to go around. It all worked out. I married the girl of my dreams and felt like Heavenly Father led my every footstep through the process. My moms picked up a daughter-in-law who would love them without condition and help in times of need. There were just too many experiences that are unexplainable any other way than to see Heavenly Father's hand in my life during that time. When I doubt the heavens are listening, I look back to the package, or the dream, or the birds, or the prayers, and all the revelatory answers that came true to the very finest detail, and I know that only a master architect could have brought all those things together in the way they came to pass. It has been so important for me to know that. Ultimately, I would need to have some serious patience and a good understanding of how to seek and receive revelation for the things that lay ahead.

CHAPTER 6

The Business of Revelation

ONE OF MY BIGGEST FEARS WAS that I would be poor. I didn't want to end up in a basement apartment with lawn chairs for furniture ever again. I didn't want to borrow money from friends or family that I knew I could never pay back. I didn't want to eat cereal with a fork to save the milk. I didn't want the life that my mom and I had through my youth. The constant strain that finances put on her when I was young was a never-ending game of catch up that left her exhausted. Once, we were so broke that she had to beg one of her brothers for a part-time job cleaning their heating and electric business on the weekends. The pay was meager and the work wasn't easy, but she did it gladly despite her constant health issues that continued to mount on top of each other like a vicious dog pile. I helped her clean occasionally, but when one of my uncles found out that I wasn't working all the time with her, he cut her pay because he had figured the hourly pay was for the two of us working simultaneously. It truly hurt her pride and her feelings. But she kept working out of pure desperation. I never wanted to be in that situation. I never wanted to beg. I never wanted to rely on a single person for my wellbeing after seeing what she went through. Also, I felt like I had something to prove. I wanted to be successful and show the world that my upbringing didn't give me some type of handicap in life, and I foolishly figured that money was the answer to gaining people's respect and admiration.

After returning from my mission, I switched my major from acting to business management to avoid becoming the "penniless actor." I absolutely loved to act, and it was always my dream to be a famous movie or Broadway star, but I knew that my chance of providing for a family was slim because I didn't have a face, voice, or body like Zac Efron and wasn't as funny and plump as Jack Black to slide by as the comic relief.

Instead of relaxing college summers with the dream job I wanted as an EFY camp counselor, I hit the streets of Utah as a door-to-door salesman working six days a week in sweltering heat. I worked my guts out. Luckily, I was good at it. I came to appreciate that I wasn't being paid for time, but for sales. If I could work smarter and harder, then I could maximize my earning potential. I shattered every sales record at the company I was working for and then kept shattering my own records.

By the time Hillary got home from her mission, I had bought a townhouse in Rexburg with a sizeable down payment and had secured a job as chief marketing officer for a multi-location pest control company that was going to pay me well into the six figures while I still had a year left of school to complete.

My desire to "not be poor" turned into a wildly stupid desire to be super rich, and I was willing to do what it took to make money, even if the work was less than enjoyable.

In total, I spent three long and hard summers selling pest control. Hillary joined me in Minneapolis to sell during the final summer before I started my role as marketing officer. The owners wanted me to put in one last summer on the doors and then transition into new responsibilities in the fall, and I thought it would be a great way for Hillary and me to travel the Midwest for a few months with some close friends.

The summer started as perfectly as it possibly could have. We were the top two salespeople in the office, and it looked like we were bound for serious sales success. We even made the decision to move back to Burley after graduation due to my job flexibility. We found a house plan we loved and wanted to get started while we wrapped up a summer of sales and our final semester of school. From the time I married Hillary until we were selling up a storm in the Twin Cities, it seemed like life was nothing but blue skies and smooth sailing ahead.

One thing I have learned is that everything can't run smoothly for too long, or life gets a little boring. Luckily for you and me, my life has never been boring, which means there is always a story to tell and there are always more pages to write.

On a sweltering day in late May, we were knocking the doors of a fresh new subdivision when Hillary said she didn't feel well. No more than thirty seconds later she ran off the porch of a house and threw up all over the freshly planted bushes, which hadn't been in the ground long enough to have their tags removed. The humor of the situation didn't escape me as I played the scenario over and over.

(Knock, knock, knock)
"Hi! I'm Hillary, and I'm here to kill all your bugs."
"Oh yeah? What type of product do you use?"

"Let me show you! *Blaaaaaaaaahhhhhhh* . . . Now don't water that bush for a few days, and I promise that *nothing* will come near it."

Before you chalk me up as an insensitive poop, you have to realize that I thought she must have just eaten something bad or been in the sun too long. I had enough experience on the doors to know that accidents happen, and they are gifts for late-night stories with friends that leave a room full of laughter even if they left a stomach empty of its contents.

There was just one problem. The nausea didn't go away after her unfortunate run-in with the bush, and I had to take her back to our apartment to rest. The next day wasn't any better. Or the next.

That was when Hillary sprang the news on me. She was pregnant.

As I sit here trying to conjure up the best words to describe what I felt when I heard the news, I have settled on *dreadfully joyful*. I was super excited to have a child with Hillary. Having children was on our Top 10 Things to Do before We Die list, but from my view, the timing could not have been worse. We were under contract to knock doors every day for three more months, and Hillary couldn't get out of bed without feeling extreme nausea. The "cover the bushes" sales approach just wouldn't work consistently enough, so we had to make the hard decision for her to stay at home.

At the same time, my sales began to slowly slip as I tried to find a balance in my new role as a husband with an extremely ill wife and working nonstop on the doors. I felt like I was working harder and smarter than I had in previous years, but I didn't like the areas I was knocking compared to my previous summers in Utah. My sales approach didn't work as well, and overall I just didn't have the same level of confidence. The combination of everything led to a less-than-stellar relationship with my bosses, and I quickly moved from the golden child of the company to a fallen star expected to have only double the sales of the next closest person in our office compared to my usual triple.

The owners were upset enough that they flew in the newly crowned golden child from a different state's office to knock in Minnesota for a week. I think their goal was to have him outsell me at all costs and prove that the area wasn't the problem, I was.

His first couple of days weren't great. He had a hard go learning the area, and I was gaining confidence that I would be able to have a "told you so" conversation with the bosses. Then he had a couple of days in a row where he outsold me and beat my best overall day in Minnesota by one account sold. That was enough of a lesson to send him back to his original territory and provide me with a big badge of shame and embarrassment compared to the motivation I am sure the owners were hoping to instill. Instead, I was mad at myself, the company, and even God. I just didn't understand why I had to go through a summer of struggles when my desire, work ethic, and obedience should have led to success. In reality, I was about to learn that my vision of the future and the success I felt owed were not the same as the heavens', and I would need to strap in for a wild ride.

As the summer ended, I was grateful to put Minnesota behind me and had high hopes that I could mend things in my new marketing role with the owners. They scheduled a kickoff meeting in order to launch some big structural changes at the company and asked that I bring Hillary along.

On our way to the meeting, our housebuilder called and asked us if we were good to move ahead with breaking ground on our house in the morning. I remember feeling a moment of panic when I said, "Yep, we're good to go!" as I realized that once the ground was plowed we were committed to a project that would cost more than all the purchases I had made in my entire life combined. I hung up, looked at Hillary, smiled, and pulled up to our meeting.

As I walked into the office, I could tell the owners were extremely nervous, which in turn left me feeling uneasy. Hillary was the only one who seemed at ease with her bubbly personality and warm smile as we exchanged pleasantries before sitting around a square table where a black binder sat purposefully closed.

As we ran out of comments on the weather meant to postpone the awkward conversation that was inevitably coming, the mood turned more intense.

I had been in enough meetings with the owners to know that this wasn't a normal meeting, which intensified my uneasiness as I searched their faces for the slightest hint as to what might be coming.

Finally, the black binder opened as they explained how the company hadn't reached the goals it had set for the summer, which in turn would affect my position. What lay before me was a new employment contract that rolled back my salary by close to 50 percent and cut commissions by even more.

As they explained the reasoning for the change, my mind drifted to thoughts on the house. I had just given the go-ahead on a project I might not be able to afford in a town I might not be able to live in. Also, with Hillary pregnant, we needed the company insurance. It became very clear that my troubles from the summer weren't left behind but were exponentially affecting me still, and I needed time to think.

I told them I didn't have an answer on the new contract and asked for twenty-four hours to get back to them, which they agreed to. As I left, my mind raced to find a solution, but all avenues seemed hopeless and led me to realize that I could sign the contract and be completely unhappy or quit and risk financial ruin and failure as a future father and provider. I was mad. Mainly at the heavens, because I felt like I had done all the right things. I had followed all the spiritual guidance and falsely felt like I was owed success and smooth life sailing for my obedience in following God's commandments. Oh, how little I knew.

As I thought over the scenarios, my wife recommended that I call my mission president, who happened to work close to where my meeting took place, and ask for his counsel along with a priesthood blessing. Luckily, he was in town and was able to make the time to meet with me.

As I walked in his office he held out his arms, which have a wingspan similar to that of an albatross, and stood ready for an embrace as he looked down at me with a warm smile and lovingly said, "Elder Ramsey, what mess have you gotten yourself into this time?"

He sat in his chair and listened intently as I told him about my situation and the dilemma I had found myself in. After I finished the story, he sat motionless for a few seconds and then snapped out of his chair and said, "Let's see what Heavenly Father has to say about it."

As he put his hands on my head and started the blessing, my mind went back to the previous blessings he had given me. As I left the mission field in England, his words guided me to navigate the rocky road that many returned missionaries face as they try to enter the real world without forgetting the valuable lessons they learned as a missionary. During my tumultuous dating life with Hillary, on more than one occasion I asked him for a blessing, and each time his words sank deep into my soul and grounded me with a firmer resolve to have faith and trust that all things will work out according to God's will and timing.

As I sat there this time, I prayed and pleaded silently that the blessing would be a similar experience to the times past. I hoped that President Munday would be inspired with the words needed to guide my troubled soul toward the solution that seemed to be eluding me. With those thoughts in my mind, he began to speak. As he talked, I felt peace.

While I don't recall all the words from this blessing, there were a couple of sentences that became cemented in my mind like traffic signals placed to guide me through a complex intersection. About halfway through, he said, "You should not stay at the pest control company. God will lead and guide you in your career choice, and you should continue with your current plans."

I couldn't believe it. After the blessing, it was so clear that I needed to quit, keep building our house in Burley, and trust that Heavenly Father would help something work out. It was quite honestly the last scenario I would have ever come up with myself. It seemed like the riskiest and least likely to succeed out of all the options. Yet I left President Munday's office feeling the peace that it was exactly what I needed to do.

I think the only people who were more shocked by my plan than I was were the owners of the pest control company. When I told them I was quitting, I practically felt their jaws drop over the phone call. Given the stress I was under, I'm sure they figured I would accept, as it was still a great amount of pay for someone just graduating and would afford me serious flexibility with my schedule and living arrangements. It was still a good offer, maybe even a great one, but it was not what I had originally signed up for.

I think it's important to add that looking back, I now understand the owners' situation. They would have been crazy to honor the first contract because it might have made the entire operation cash-poor based on the overall company's position after the summer. I also was no longer the star salesperson.

For them, they did what they had to do to keep their company moving forward, and I landed in the crosshairs of that. On the other hand, I had to be in a place I could thrive and feel confident in, and that was no longer possible for me as an employee of that organization. The owners have more than made it up to me since then. But at the time, it was brutal.

I quit my job, broke ground on the house in Burley, and went back to Rexburg with Hillary for a final semester of school. I had no idea what I was going to do with the rest of my life or how it was all going to come together. The only thing I understood was that to get me through the unknown I needed to have faith that Heavenly Father did have a plan for me and everything that happened over the previous six months was for a very specific purpose.

Each day of my last semester was a frantic study to try and determine what passions I wanted to pursue for a career. A majority of my classes centered on different aspects of marketing, and one area in particular that was proving to pique my interest was all things internet.

I had a class called B250, and the whole point of the course was to start an online business and sell something during the semester. I found every lesson fascinating! At the same time, I was taking a course on computer programming, and the combining result meant that I could fiddle around with HTML and hack together a website for an e-commerce business. As I thought about what I might sell online, I tried to think of things that were immediately available in my surrounding area to cut down on any transportation costs and ended up settling on a good ol' Idaho potato. Not just any Idaho potato, but the big ones. Ones that were larger than a pound a piece. I figured that there were enough people who wanted novelty gifts that I could offer them five-, twenty-, and fifty-pound boxes through a basic website and get at least a few sales. So I hacked together the website, and HugeIdahoPotato.com was up and running. Through a few lessons in the class I learned the basics about online advertising on Google and tested the theories on my extremely simple and ugly website with great success. Within a few weeks, I had made two hundred dollars shipping potatoes across the United States, and I was hungry to learn more.

At that time, I was also looking at the possibilities of starting my own pest control company. It was a business I knew well and felt I could be successful with. I dreaded the idea of knocking more doors but knew that I would be willing to do whatever it would take to make things work.

Ultimately, I decided that I needed to take my ideas to Heavenly Father, and I knew the temple was the best place to accomplish that. So I went and sat in the celestial room and began to pray. I thought about everything that had happened over the summer and the blessing I had received from President Munday. Then I pondered starting an internet marketing agency, which I had no idea how to start and very little idea how to perform the work, or a pest control company, which seemed like a very safe and secure bet that I knew I could be successful in.

In order to capture the most accurate representation of what happened next, I am going to share an entry from my journal dated September 16, 2008.

> I went to the temple today and was taught a lot about faith and revelation. When Adam was a lone man in the wilderness, the first thing he did was call upon God. God answered and guided him. Today, I prayed about our house and was told we would have enough to cover ourselves. Also, I was told that as I have hearkened to God, I would be told the career path

I should take. Today Heavenly Father made known unto me that I should move home and start an internet marketing firm. I was told that success would come fast and that I would bring people into Burley to help the economy and also that we would become prominent in our field. That businesses large and small would seek us out to learn.

I felt that I shouldn't pursue setting up a pest control company and focus on learning as much as possible about online marketing. I was told that we would be successful very fast and to not worry about house finances. I was told hard times would come, but I should have the faith to press on and rely on what I had learned while in the temple. At that point, in my mind I saw the business start out in my home and then progress to be in a nice building in Burley. That is where the vision in my mind ended.

I need to be believing I know I heard the voice of the Spirit like I have so many times before. My problem has been to second-guess myself and not trust in the Lord's miracles. Currently, I know literally nothing of web development and internet marketing. But with God with me anything is possible.

I left the temple that day and went to work to make that vision a reality.

The next few years flew by like a gazelle being chased by a very hungry lion. It was a frantic run across unsteady ground with a constant feeling that I was fighting against the clock to be successful (and avoid being eaten). I would grab phone books and call businesses throughout Idaho and Utah to try and drum up business. I networked through friends and family to find out if anyone needed a website or online marketing. Slowly but surely, a few clients started to come out of the woodworks. It was enough business and money to scrape by on, but nowhere near enough to fulfill the vision I remembered so vividly.

In order to improve my skills and under desperation to grow the business, I signed up for an online forum where other digital marketers discussed everything under the sun. One of the threads was specifically to introduce yourself and share your personal company website so that others could offer feedback.

My website got torched! Everyone said it was awful. Comment after comment was worse than the one before, as if people were getting more confidence to offer brutal honesty because the person before them did the same.

As I read through the comments, it became quite clear that I might not have been meant for the industry, and I really started to doubt my future in it. While I was wallowing in my own self-pity, I received a private message from a well-respected individual in the community that changed my approach to everything.

"You offer search engine optimization, web design, and paid advertising. That is exactly the same as hundreds of thousands of companies around the world, who, by the look of things, do better than you at it. What can you be the best at? What can you become known for?"

The comment hit me like a ton of bricks. Well, a survivable ton of bricks. I knew he was right. At that time, there was no reason to use my company compared to any other. So I thought through what it was that I could specialize in and truly become known for. As I went through my client list, one of the areas that they all had in common was that they were local businesses who needed to show up on Google Maps services. I looked online and realized there was only a handful of people focusing on that specific industry, and it became very clear that I needed to join their ranks. One of the more prolific bloggers in local maps was a man named David Mihm. He was a very smart marketer from Portland who had dismantled Google's local map algorithm and was getting national attention for his work. Deciding that I had nothing to lose, I wrote an email to David Mihm on August 7, 2009, and asked him how I could become an expert in the local search field. He responded, "The best advice I can give you is to optimize the local listings of a bunch of clients. The more you "play" in the space, the better you'll get at teasing out the parts of the algorithm that really matter."

Beyond that, he gave me a list of blogs and websites to follow. I immediately dove into every one of the sites and learned everything I possibly could about local search. I took notes, and then I started testing my own theories and expanding on what had been written.

While doing that, I realized the most valuable networking lesson I ever learned was to simply share. I started blogging, which led to me being a guest writer on many popular marketing websites, and I attended a few small conferences, one of which was the first ever GetListed: Local University. I offered to help any way that I could and ended up checking people in at the badge station.

Fast forward to this day, and I am a LocalU faculty member and part-owner of the conference series. I have spoken at events big and small across the world, and like my original revelation said, we became prominent in our field, and businesses large and small sought us out to learn. We have brought over twenty-five people into our community and restored a big building downtown to house our operation. All of this happened in little ol' Burley, Idaho. The most non-tech, non-progressive, agriculture-focused area in Southern Idaho. My business, Nifty Ventures, has been on the Inc. 5000 list three times for being one of the fastest-growing companies in America.

None of the events happened because I am special or super smart. I simply received an answer from the heavens about what I should do, and I went to work doing it. I trusted in the revelation. I became passionate about the local search marketing space and was willing to share information and help others learn how it all works. Almost every client we have at Nifty comes as a referral from clients, friends, blog posts, webinars, and conferences. Not one client ever came from a cold call.

I will forever be in debt to David Mihm and the rest of the local search community for showing me the ropes and how to serve others in business compared to just myself. I am most thankful to Heavenly Father for lighting the path ahead for me enough to have confidence to pursue.

I have found that receiving revelation is hard business, but it is absolutely key to being a member of The Church of Jesus Christ of Latter-day Saints. It's hard to know what comes from God and what comes from us or other sources. Acting on the right revelation is even harder. From the experiences I had with dating and marrying Hillary to starting my company, I became absolutely focused on following the heaven-given guidance. Every revelation to this point in my life had come to pass exactly as I was told it would. I felt unstoppable. I felt like I knew the truth to the point of my life. I had a bright vision of hope for the future and knew where I stood with God. This, for me, was the most important aspect of being a member of the Church and continuing forward in faith. I trusted God, and though I still wasn't ready or willing to seek answers by diving into my past and the confusion that surrounded my faith and my family, I hoped to continue to receive guidance about my future. Is revelation real? Yes. I know it because I experienced it firsthand. In the cases of my marriage and business, I have no idea where I would be without the guidance I received.

Not every story regarding revelation always has such exact fulfillment as the previous experiences. Nor do they have such happy endings. I look at receiving revelation a lot like lifting weights. You like the idea of working out, but it's super hard to get enough desire to show up at the gym. Once you are there, the weights are heavy. They naturally want to stay on the ground, due to a wonderful thing called gravity, and are opposed to being picked up over and over. It makes your body hurt a little more with every rep and takes more resolve to follow through. True strength is created by that opposition over the long haul—not just one day of lifting, but over and over. Spiritual strength works the exact same way. Everyone likes the idea of being led by God and receiving revelation, but it's hard to be humble enough to seek, and once you seek it can be brutal to follow through on the answers received. It can hurt. It can be in exact opposition to your will. It can tear your spiritual muscles to the core, all so that you can be strengthened. With that in mind, it would be unfair for me to skip over the "hard times will come, but you should have the faith to press on" aspect of revelation I received in the temple before starting Nifty.

I have had many revelations that left me broken, doubtful, or confused. Without such strong, positive past experiences, I don't know if I could have spiritually survived the hard ones.

When I was new to revelation, my view on the feelings, thoughts, and words that came to my mind were very black and white. I thought that following revealed guidance led to perfect fulfillment and happy outcomes. Now my expectations are not as naive. My faith is different—deeper, but different in the fact that I no longer think that following Heavenly Father is ever a walk on the easiest path. On the contrary, I find that it may be a straight path, but it's often one with thorns, boulders, mud, and fog that can slow you to a crawl, and the only thing that will be able to keep you going is your knowledge that it is simply your personal command from God to do so. The business of receiving and acting on revelation is one of the hardest businesses to be in. I have spent years trying to understand God's will for my life and have tried to do my best to follow His words. Getting to a point that you can truly say, "Not my will, but Thine, be done," is the ultimate goal, and I find that when I feel like I am getting closer, the command adds a little more weight to ensure that the opposition leads to strengthening and not carelessness. It is worth it. It's hard, but I hope you can see through the stories shared throughout this book that a life of trying to follow revelation from Heavenly Father is better than one trying to manage it on your own. After all, it's through patience and revelation that I was finally able to begin understanding my mother.

CHAPTER 7

Learning to Love the Sinner

MY MOM'S BIGGEST FEAR WHEN I left for my mission was that I would come back intolerant. She feared that instead of returning with a heart full of love toward all people, I would become like the Sadducees and Pharisees of old and boast in my own holiness while condemning her way of life.

I wish that I could say that was far from the truth, but it wasn't.

I loved my mission in England and the people I met. I served them, taught them, and saw what they could become. Each day, I studied my scriptures and read great talks, pondered the meaning of it all, and connected dots that some spend a lifetime searching for. In all, I came home with a deep knowledge of the Church's doctrine and a deep desire to convince my mom that I had all the answers to life. Though I did gain an extensive amount of knowledge, I still had a serious lack of wisdom.

It didn't take long for conversations with my mom to turn to religion upon my return. It seemed that no matter the subject discussed, it would always come back to homosexuality, which was something that we could *never* talk about before my mission. Now it was the central focus in every debate.

I would try to dodge the bullets and questions that my mom would throw my way as she tried to peel back the layers of the things I said. Deep down, I think she knew where I stood and wanted me to just say it completely forthright and out loud.

My big secret that I kept deep within my soul was that I absolutely, 100 percent hated that my mom was a homosexual. I hated that she was in a relationship with a woman. I hated that I had to explain it to people. I hated that I had to hide it from others. I hated that my mom made a choice to have a partner. I hated that I didn't have a dad, and it had always been her fault. Homosexuality had been the base cause of my mom not being part of the religion that I came to believe in with my whole heart. Homosexuality had been the reason I was uncomfortable having friends over, it was the reason I moved out, it was the reason I never wanted to bring girlfriends around. Homosexuality had been the reason I didn't have the normal life that I dreamed of, and even after serving a mission, I couldn't admit my feelings to myself, let alone someone else, and even dream of being able to forgive her for it.

My hope and mission after returning from England was to talk the homosexuality out of my mom with doctrine, spirituality, faith, and prayers. Homosexuality was the problem holding my family back. I believed that homosexuality was one of the absolute worst of sins. Why? Not because of something I read or something that someone taught me, but because of the life I lived. My enmity for homosexuality came from the time so many years ago when I lay on the floor and stared at the ceiling feeling like everything in my world was broken and backward. I didn't understand, and I wanted to. I didn't know why things had to be different after that day.

I don't think that my viewpoint was all that different from other Latter-day Saints who have husbands, wives, brothers, sisters, or children who "came out." I've even heard people say that they think the death of a loved one would be better than finding out that person is gay. Imagine that for a minute. Death. The absolute end of life on earth. Now, I know what they were *really* saying was that they would rather see a loved one die living what they deemed a "righteous life" compared to living in a way they thought might jeopardize their eternal salvation in heaven. Latter-day Saints don't look at death as the end. But death? That is a strong level of hate and fear toward *anything*.

I remember one particular day, after a religious conversation that left my mom in tears, Tina came to talk to me. She never was one to talk deeply about things. Especially religion. That day was different, and she had a request that I not talk to my mom about religion or homosexuality anymore. It hurt my mom too much. Tina wasn't mean about it. It was more of a plea. As I looked into Tina's eyes, I could see that she really cared for my mom. She loved her. She was trying to protect her. I had never seen that so clearly before. At that moment I had a thought. A revelation came into my mind that I simply couldn't shake. The love and patience Tina had for my mom was seventy times seven purer than mine. I wondered how that could be. After all, I was the churchy one. I was the one who studied biblical love and served a mission. I knew the doctrine. I knew how to follow God's words and strive to constantly be better, and *they* were gay!

I told her I would try my best. As I left, I didn't feel the joy of triumph from an argument won. I felt sick. I felt . . . angry. As I tried to find justification for the situation, I was left with the powerful and overwhelming thought that the Savior never felt sick and angry after talking about His gospel. The outcome of that revelation was too much for me to handle. So I bottled everything back up and cut any reference to homosexuality or religion out of conversations with my mom. I felt like a lit match trying to avoid burning down a dried forest. I figured that avoidance was the best policy, and that idea carried me through the next several years of life, marriage, and a couple of kids, all while largely keeping a certain level of distance between my feelings and my mom.

Homosexuality was simply too hard for me to deal with. The feelings were too deep, and I was not ready to address them.

/////

As the years passed by and my business and family seemed to double every twenty-four months, along with the challenges of both, the stresses of life caught up to me in a way I couldn't imagine.

It started with the revelation I received in the temple about starting Nifty on September 16, 2008. I omitted one sentence from the story earlier in order to share the details now. In my journal I wrote:

> I was told that success would come fast and that I would bring people to Burley to help the economy and also that I would be prominent in that field. That businesses large and small would seek me out to learn. ***I was told that while doing this I would be called as a bishop for my church.***

The revelation I received about starting Nifty was specific. I needed to move to Burley. The business would be successful, and companies would seek us out. The part about being called as a bishop caught me completely off guard. It had nothing to do with the revelation I was seeking but instantly seemed like the overarching purpose behind everything. I needed to be in Burley to be a bishop. That was what my Heavenly Father wanted from me, and Nifty would get me back there to make it happen.

For those reading without a flair for Latter-day Saint phraseology, a bishop is a non-paid position that rotates in a local congregation roughly every five years. The bishop is chosen by the stake president, who seeks revelation and prays earnestly to know who God would have him call. It's a very special process in our church. You don't ask for the calling. You don't put an application in. You are not paid. You are chosen. It takes roughly twenty to forty hours a week in your off time. You are basically responsible for running everything. People come to you with their struggles, sins, and weaknesses, and you counsel with them. Ultimately, the work of teaching the youth and adults and determining what responsibilities everyone has in a congregation falls on the shoulders of a bishop. It's a hard responsibility, but it is very respected within the Church.

I locked the feelings and revelation on being called away in a deep part of my soul and went about life building Nifty. As the years passed by, I saw an absolute exact fulfillment of the vision I had as it related to the business. You could say that "it came to pass." Then, in 2009, our local bishop of the Burley Eighth Ward was called to be the stake president. As I sat there and heard his name called, the experience from the temple came flooding back to my mind, and I immediately began to feel a tingle all over my body. The feeling came again that I would be called as a bishop. I looked at my wife, and she looked at me at the exact same time. I could tell that whatever experience I was having had trickled over to her as well.

I spent the next week examining my life. I thought about every reason why I was a horrible choice to be bishop. Every sin, misstep, and shortcoming played like a broken record through my mind. Hours passed as slowly as trees grow while I stayed on my knees making peace with Heavenly Father and myself to be prepared.

When I walked in the chapel the next week at church, I saw the newly called stake presidency on the stand and knew that something was off. As they started the meeting, they made the announcement of who the new bishop was going to be.

It definitely wasn't me.

I immediately began to play the experience I had in the temple over and over in my mind. I also thought back to the previous week, when the feeling came again during stake conference. My heart sank. I figured either I messed up or what I was calling "revelation" was simply made-up nonsense in my mind. The experience affected me enough that I decided to meet with the stake president for a blessing and get any advice he could offer on the situation.

As I sat in his office, he told me that when he was set apart by Elder Oaks he was given some advice that he found odd. He stated, "There are many brethren that probably had the feeling that they could be called as the stake president. Heavenly Father gives them this experience for them to know that they were worthy, or to help them examine and prepare for the future." He also told me the story of Nephi's vision in which Nephi said, "I know that [God] loveth his children; nevertheless, I do not know the meaning of all things" (1 Nephi 11:17).

While I didn't necessarily feel like I had a full answer or closure as to why the revelatory experience that I had didn't come to pass exactly like I saw with Nifty, I left his office feeling comfort in the visit. As I walked out, the stake president told me to ensure that I offered my wife a blessing, as she was struggling with the confusion from the experience as well.

When I got home, I did as instructed and gave my wife a blessing.

I've given hundreds of blessings. Sometimes the words come easily. Sometimes words are a little vague. Sometimes it's like pulling teeth for words to come at all. While I will not share everything from the experience, I can definitely classify this blessing as one that will go down in both of our memories forever. Words and inspiration flowed freely. One part stood out in particular. The blessing said, "The reason that you and your husband had these feelings and experiences is to prepare you for the future, for in five years there will be a call to serve as bishop."

After the words were said, we both had a surreal feeling of peace and clarity that seemed to last for days. There was no doubt in our minds that this came from our Heavenly Father. We'd seen many blessings fulfilled and had absolute faith that this was the answer and explanation we were seeking. Everything made sense again. Everything had its purpose and reason.

But those feelings didn't last forever.

Reality set in very quickly, and it seemed like the peace that I had gave way to constant feelings of inadequacy, doubt, and anger. It was back to a game of patience, one that would prove much harder than waiting for my call or waiting for Hillary to return from a mission. Five years is a long time to have something constantly on your mind that guides your every action.

As the years passed, Nifty continued to flourish. But while that happened, everything at church became much harder. I analyzed everything to death—who were in specific callings and responsibilities, what people thought about me, what I had done (or not done) to ensure that I wouldn't hold back the fulfillment of the blessing from becoming reality. The roller coaster was constant and completely exhausting. One particular experience about gave me a heart attack.

When we moved into our house, we figured it was about a five-year plan, and then we would move. After our revelatory experience, though, I was petrified to leave because that would change the congregation we were in, and in my opinion at the time, that would throw off God's plan for us.

On Christmas in 2013, there was a ward boundary change. Basically, you are assigned the church you go to based on where you live. In cities outside of Idaho and Utah, a ward boundary might be the entire metropolis or even county. In Burley, it's mere street blocks. Our neighborhood was all together in one ward, and they split the ward directly between our house and my brother-in-law and sister-in-law's house. Our shared yard became the division between the two wards.

I did my best to put away the hard thoughts and anxiety that seemed to be ever-present and just dive into the new ward with a better mindset and willingness to serve. I loved it. I served in the Young Men organization, where I felt truly happy and fulfilled at church for the first time in years. Overall, what started out as a hard change in wards seemed to have been just the opposite. I felt more at home, more connected, and more focused on others instead of myself.

In 2014, the time came again for a new bishop to be called. This time, I was absolutely sure it was going to be me. After all, there was the blessing and there were countless other revelatory experiences that seemed to align everything. I had literally thought about it and what I would do for five long years. I had my counselors chosen. I had my suits dry-cleaned. I felt ready to take on the challenges that Heavenly Father was placing in front of me.

As a side note, I think it is important to state that I didn't want to be the bishop for glory's sake. I simply wanted to follow the revelation I received and be pointed down the right path, the path that God had for me. In the *Lectures on Faith*, Joseph Smith taught that it took three things "to exercise faith in God unto life and salvation":

"First, the idea that he actually exists;

"Secondly, a correct idea of his character, perfections, and attributes;

"Thirdly, an actual knowledge that the course of life which one is pursuing is according to His will."[1]

I desperately clung to the third point. I wanted to know without question that the course I was pursuing was God's will and being called as bishop was what I equated to an answer to that question.

I remember seeing the stake president on the stand, which wasn't an uncommon sight every few weeks. But when he stood and walked to the pulpit, he gripped it with both hands and paused before he released the previous bishopric and thanked them for their service. Then he read the name of the new bishop.

My thoughts went back to that moment when I was ten. The day after my mom told me she was a lesbian. When my world stopped making sense. I lay on the floor in my grandpa's office and stared at the ceiling. I was so hurt and lost and broken that all I could do was shout at the heavens and wonder where my God was.

The name read was my next-door neighbor and good friend. I had him down on my short list for counselors. I couldn't make it through the rest of church. I went home. I lay on the floor and stared at the ceiling.

This might seem so insignificant to some. People have loved ones die, spouses who leave, financial ruin, and a never-ending list of bad things happen that make them doubt their purpose and their faith. But regardless of what traumatic event "breaks"

---

1   "Lecture 3," in *The Lectures on Faith in Historical Perspective*, ed. Larry E. Dahl and Charles D. Tate Jr. (Provo, UT: Religious Studies Center, Brigham Young University), 65–73.

a person and brings them to their knees, I believe we all have something that shatters certain misconceptions of our faith and self-worth at some point in our lives. There will be something that will make you wonder where God is, why He doesn't seem to care, and if you are completely alone.

This was my breaking point.

It was the point that I doubted the existence of a loving God and continuing revelation in my life. I doubted myself. I was so sure of the blessing and my experiences that it became the core of who I was and what my beliefs were founded on. If I were called as bishop, it would have proven that God was there, He reveals things to His children, and everything was real. I felt like it would show that I was right to come back to church and solidify that He led me over the previous difficult years. If it didn't happen, then it was all a big sham or I was a big failure. It was all black and white in my mind. No room for grey. No room for question.

To make matters worse, it is so taboo to mention a desire to serve as bishop even if it came about due to what I thought was absolutely clear revelation. I felt like I couldn't tell anyone about it. So I suffered in silence.

As the days went on, I slipped further and further into a dark hole. I didn't care about my business (after all, it was part of the revelation that stated that I would build Nifty in Burley so I could serve as a bishop). I felt like an absolute failure to my wife. I figured that my lack of call must have been something I did. I must have sinned too much. I figured I had not been faithful enough. I said the wrong things. It was as if in a single instant my imperfections had damned me, and I was left alone.

My mind quickly went to some very hard absolutes. The process went something like this: I received revelation, and it didn't come to pass; therefore God lied. God cannot lie, or He ceases to be God; therefore there is no God. The Church isn't true. My whole life is a big fat lie.

It's like I forgot everything positive, every fulfilled blessing, revelation, and experience that had led me through the previous years and comprise the beginning chapters of this book. They are amazing, faith-promoting stories, but all I had space for in my mind was this vicious darkness that clouded everything in front of and behind me.

As the days, months, and years went on, I withdrew in all aspects of my life. Work, family, friends, church. I still went to things; I just wasn't fully "there." My mind was always off fighting a constant inner battle. My confidence was shot because I no longer felt like I knew who I was. Simply put, I was mad at a God I could hardly believe in, and I felt abandoned and forsaken by the only Father I felt like I could rely on. It was as if I had reverted back to the lost little ten-year-old who was angry and alone, staring at the ceiling struggling to understand why. My love and patience seemed like they were hanging by a very small thread. To give a truly accurate depiction of where I was, I am copying some journal entries from those times.

June 25, 2015

I have been so negative lately and find myself slipping into anger, unhappiness, and largely I just have bad thoughts and make brash decisions and actions about everything. As I prayed, I felt Heavenly Father's forgiveness along with the statement "As oft as you repent you will be forgiven." Again, Heavenly Father recounted the struggles He knows I am facing and mentioned that not only are sins forgiven, but weaknesses are not sins and can be humbling and we can find comfort through the heavens.

I prayed that I might have strength. I feel so lost still and just want to be happy and know that the path I am on is right.

For me, I can't deny that my most recent long-term depression is tied to the revelation I received about 5.5 years ago that I would be called to be the bishop in 5 years. It's been a major roller coaster since that time. I have wondered if I have failed and if I wouldn't be called due to things happening around me. Then, when a new bishop was called, I felt devastated and ultimately like I had completely failed at whatever test I was currently in. After all, I have had countless experiences telling me that I would serve in 5 years. As I thought through these things again (as I do many times in prayer or meditation), I felt again the story of Nephi and Samuel the Lamanite [stories from the Book of Mormon]. Five years came and went where the people were looking for a sign in the heavens of the Savior's birth, and the people began to be very sorrowful, lest by any means those things which had been spoken might not come to pass. But they did come to pass.

April 15, 2016

Near the end of 2015, I figured the clock had run out of time on the revelation to be fulfilled. I am left standing, wondering why I can't let this go and why it matters so much to my soul. I have honestly lost track of how many times I have prayed and how much revelation I have received on being called as the bishop. There has yet to be a single time in prayer where the revelation is that it was the wrong time, or I was wrong, or I wasn't worthy. On the contrary, every time I feel like it's coming soon. Or it's just around the corner. But corner after corner has shown me that it is not the case.

This past Tuesday I was at the temple. I didn't want to go. I'm tired and seriously running out of hope and faith. But I went. When I got there, the session was full, so I left completely broken and spent the next 2 hours wandering aimlessly, trying to decide if I would go back for the later session or not. The stories of Nephi, and Ammon, and Abinadi, and Alma flashed through my mind, and they all went something like this . . .

"We were depressed and beaten, but the Lord commanded us to do something, so we found the strength to press on, then the miracle came."

I went back to the session. As I got into the celestial room, I felt as if I were carrying the burdens of all the previous years of pain and anguish that had come with feeling like God had sent me on a wild goose chase that has cost me my faith, hope, and happiness. I read some scriptures until I was basically the only one left in the celestial room, and then I prayed. I prayed my heart out. Yet again, I felt the all-too-familiar whisper of the Spirit that it would be fulfilled very soon.

I think Hillary and I are so desperate at this point that it is becoming harder to know if our will is coming through in thoughts or if it is the will of the Lord. Overall, I can think of nothing good that has come from this experience. At first, it helped to push me to be better. For the first 5 years. Sure, there were times of serious doubt and struggle, but I had faith it would come to pass, and I pushed myself so hard to be ready. The past 2 years, though, have been a repeated feeling of damnation. I feel a combination of despair and anger and hopelessness that the life Heavenly Father foreordained me for is on a path that I am not.

Nothing has or would give me more pleasure than to spend my life in service knowing that I was on the path God wanted me to be on and accomplishing the things I have been meant to do. Instead, through all of my prayer, scripture study, and thoughts, I am left feeling like a piece of my soul is damaged and broken. I don't have the complete faith, hope, and charity I once had. I don't feel confident in the future. I don't feel love for myself. I don't feel the love of God for me. Sundays leave me feeling hurt and sorrowful.

I feel close to the point where if I don't have more faith-building experiences I am going to be unable to rebound from this. I have spent a lifetime battling against all the reasons people have for why the Church isn't true or why there is no

God, and now I am up against the very center core belief that has gotten me through everything:

Does revelation exist today?

April 18, 2016

I know it's only been a few days since I last wrote, but how hard of days they have been. I have felt more defeated and hopeless in the last few days than I have in a long time. I feel like everything is at a tipping point. Hillary is pregnant and hardly able to move. I am quick to get angry, slow to pray, and even slower to show forth the Christlike attributes I know are important.

This is what depression feels like. The best way to explain it is the feeling that you can see exactly what you want your life to be like, but you have very little to no control over accomplishing that. Your mind is stuck in the past with no hope for the future. I know that I can do better, but I literally don't have the strength. I am in a battle with my mind almost all day long about where either I or Heavenly Father went wrong, and I am just tired.

How many more days will this absolute hell continue? Is there ever peace from it? Is there ever a day where I can have my faith and reconcile this situation, or is the only peace to shut it all out of my mind?

As you can clearly see, I was a complete mess. Maybe not on the same level as Miley Cyrus and her wrecking ball, but I was definitely not myself. The little boy who lay in the office and held on to his anger for survival through the years seemed to have complete control of me. All he wanted to know was . . . Why?

I eventually worked up the courage to talk to the stake president. He recommended a book and gave me his copy to read. It was called *Hearing the Voice of the Lord* by Gerald Lund. All of my issues were centered on my ability to receive revelation. Feeling like that part of me was broken and struggling with depression left me unable to make decisions and constantly feeling stuck. As I started to read the book, I found myself gaining truths about the revelatory process. I also began to feel a small level of hope that even though I didn't understand the experience I had, the feelings were undeniably from God and someday I would understand them. In the meantime, I gained confidence that it was okay to seek revelation in prayer again and continue to learn how the Spirit speaks to me.

There wasn't a moment in time that I saw things change dramatically for the better. It was just a daily thing. Slowly yet surely, I was coming out of a deep void and pressing forward. I still had questions, and I still had struggles. But ultimately, I was starting to have some positive experiences again with asking, seeking, knocking, and receiving answers.

It was in this state that I started to notice a change slowly working inside of me. It was as if my ability to perceive others struggling increased tenfold. I could look at someone and say, "I know exactly what you are going through because I've been there, and quite frankly, I am not totally through it."

This new understanding led me to look at people in a completely new light. Where I might condemn someone for their actions before due to my black-and-white view of the world, I now began to try and understand what brought them to that gray point in their life. Instead of distancing myself from doubters, I realized how easy it is to be shaken, even when you think it is impossible. Overall, I began to be empathetic toward the struggle. What is the struggle? It's everyone's individual Achilles' heel. It could be doubt, sin, weakness, pride, trauma, or any other aspect that brings someone to the brink of giving up.

I knew what it was like to find the truth when you felt a void before, but now I finally understood what it was like to believe in something wholeheartedly and then have your foundation challenged to the core.

With that lens on, I started looking around at people, and what I saw shocked me. Everyone was battling something. Some battled depression, some anger, some doubt, some sin, but if I looked hard enough there was always something deep down inside that brought them great amounts of fear, sorrow, anger, or shame. Something they wished they didn't have to deal with and wanted very few people to know about.

Then, I finally saw my mother.

From a very young age, my mother lived a life full of the hardest struggles. She didn't grow up having a great relationship with her parents or siblings. Older boys took advantage of her in her youth, and men had belittled her as an adult. She felt nothing but judgment and contempt by many Church members throughout her life. She didn't know how to deal with strong feelings of attraction to women for years, or why she had them, or where they came from. She didn't ask for it. She didn't ask for a strained relationship with my father. She didn't desire to get pregnant.

Despite all her early challenges and missteps, and in the face of impossible odds, she finished her education and became a great teacher and voice for those whom society didn't have a place for. She also did her absolute best to raise me with as much love and support as any parent in her situation could. Was she perfect? No. But did she give me her all? Yes.

Beyond raising me, she also tried to see the good in the average person while assuming that she wouldn't get acceptance in return, due to being a lesbian. I never witnessed her purposefully hurt another human out of spite, fear, or uncertainty. I rarely heard her speak ill of people in general, unless she felt they were causing harm to others. She gave people the benefit of the doubt.

When her health failed her, she moved back to the town she swore she wouldn't return to in order for me to have friends and family around to help. From the time I was born, her life had been a series of sacrifices, and she gave up her will for my best interest over and over again. Could anything more be asked of a mother? Yet I had spent so much of my life covered in my own anger and shame that I couldn't see the sacrifices made, and I didn't appreciate her acceptance of the life I chose to live. In return for everything she had done for me, I had never offered her my acceptance, and I didn't know what it would take to do so. Then I found out.

We were at Tina's family reunion in Jackson Hole, Wyoming, when my mom received a phone call from her doctor. She had gone in for an annual checkup the week before, and they found a large lump they wanted to biopsy "just to be safe." The doctor told her she had an aggressive form of breast cancer and would need to begin treatments immediately.

She had been through so many medical problems already, and I couldn't believe that cancer was going to be added to the list. As all of us tried to cope with the news, I watched in awe as she was still able to laugh and joke with everyone around. Instead of people giving her comfort, it seemed reversed, and she had to be the one to comfort others about her own cancer.

Just before starting treatments, she asked for a blessing from me. I don't think I have ever put as much into being able to give her a blessing as I did for that one. As I placed my hands on her head, I didn't feel condemnation or judgment for her life as a lesbian. I felt God's love, God's trust. I felt His hope and sorrow for the hard life she had lived. His words truly flowed through me. He shared things in the blessing that I hadn't thought of or heard before. It was the first moment in time where I saw my mom through God's eyes. I saw her as His and Mother in Heaven's daughter. Both. I knew that she was Their child. She was loved. And she was gay.

It's been a part of her for as long as she can remember. It's caused monumental challenges in her life. But it's her. I had spent so much of my life focused on my issues with and shame for having a gay mother that I had never stopped to consider how hard her road has been as she simply tried to do the best she could with the life she was given. She didn't ask to be attracted to women. In a black-and-white world, she was dealt a gray hand from the very beginning.

I thought back to my deepest, darkest secret: my true hatred for homosexuality and what it had done to my family and me. I realized that I didn't hate homosexuality, nor did I hate the people. I hated my shame about being the son of a lesbian. I hated the fear that I was being judged, or looked down on, or passed over because being gay was too different for people to understand. I hated that I didn't feel comfortable, and I didn't feel proud of my moms and what they did for me over the years despite the difficulties. I hated that we hid from the world. I hated that my family was different.

That is when I received the most important revelation in my life. I needed to learn how to love and forgive myself. The sinner.

I had spent a lifetime wishing I wasn't who I was. Wishing that I didn't have a Muslim dad who didn't even know I existed and a lesbian mom. But that was God's gift to me to become what I am today. If I take the gay out of my mom, I wouldn't be the same person, nor would she. I started out jealous, envious, and covetous of others. I was always angry. I was always judging. I was a Pharisee. I wanted the praise and acceptance of man instead of God, who loved my mom and me for exactly who we were from the beginning. I wanted to appear to the world to be perfect, with a perfect nuclear family, and have a perfect childhood. I didn't see at the time that the imperfections made me who I am—a strong, passionate, caring fighter—and the imperfections both my mom and I have are a beautiful gift to learn patience, love, and empathy.

What was the outcome of this revelation? This book. The elimination of shame. The openness to talk about what I wanted to keep hidden. A newfound love, respect, and understanding for my mother and her homosexuality. The ability to accept the life I have been given and accept others' walks of life as well.

///// /

When my mom started her chemotherapy treatments and her health began to falter, it became apparent that she was going to need assistance on a daily basis, and she moved in with us.

As I helped her unpack, I couldn't help but think about the lost time we had from the years I moved out. Now she was going to be with my family every day, making new memories that would replace some of the ones that might be best to forget.

A week after she moved in, we had our fourth child, Griffin, who came into the world looking just like his dad with big hands, a chubby face, and dimples. This time around, my mom didn't have to be in Logan to finish her schooling, and she got to watch Griffin grow through that first year of his life that she missed with me. I watched her hold him close and see some of his first smiles. She cheered him on in his first steps.

Each day led to new memories, and eventually to long-overdue conversations about our relationship. I was able to finally express to her the struggles I faced growing up. As I shared, she cried.

My mom battled and beat her cancer. Through the process, I came to see and know her for the truly wonderful, loving, fun, and gay mother she is.

While my mom lived with us, each day my kids would wake up a little too early and sneak down to Nana's room. They have Nana (Janet, my mom) and Nina (Tina). Nana let them in for morning cuddles and gave them candy to ensure she's their favorite. She comes to all their activities, loves to take them to the latest movies, and lives to spoil them. It's her reward after the struggles of raising me.

Recently, my nine-year-old son asked me what it meant to be gay. He said he heard the word at school because of how he crossed his legs. I told him it's when boys like boys, and girls like girls. He immediately piped up, "Like Nana and Nina?"

I said yes and explained that some people have those feelings and that we really don't know why they have them, but as Latter-day Saints, we need to love everyone even if they are different from how we are. I asked him if he had any more questions.

He looked at me and said, "Not really, but I will let you know if I do."

He was the same age that I was when I had found out, and he took the information as casually as if I had told him that Nana had grey hair. He didn't lie on the floor and stare at the ceiling. He didn't curse the heavens. He didn't have shame. He just loved his grandparents.

I don't know what the future holds for him or my other kids and their opinions on homosexuality. But I couldn't help but see the dramatic contrast between our experiences of finding out my mom was a lesbian. It's like the upcoming generations are born with more tolerance, empathy, and understanding than the previous. Maybe his will be the generation that finds a way for religion and homosexuality to create a beautiful common ground that all can be comfortable with.

When my mom moved in with us, initially I think I secretly hoped it would be her path back to the Church. What was interesting was watching how well my mom was doing being surrounded by my kids while Tina was all alone in a house a few miles away. My mom was happy, Tina was depressed. I first thought that maybe Heavenly Father was guiding them apart, but it sure didn't seem like both were better off.

As our house became more cramped with growing kids and the stairs began to be more difficult for my mom to scale, we made plans to move to a bigger house. We looked high and low and planned on living on the Snake River, but absolutely nothing worked. We wanted to find a house with a little more land and build a granny pad for my mom. We tried to move for over two years and went through over ten different projects that fell through in one way or another. Then, as I wrestled with Heavenly Father to figure out why nothing seemed to fall into place, Tina came into my mind.

I had been taking care of my mom and we had done a lot of healing with our relationship, but my plans didn't involve Tina. She and my mom were still extremely close, but at the time there was no adequate way to define their relationship. They had been together and lived in the same house for over twenty years but had never legally married in the state of Idaho. They had their rough patches like many couples do, and it left things a little up in the air during my mom's battle with cancer. Basically, they wanted to be together but just not live together. That is when I found a duplex along the Snake River. I had a wild thought enter my mind: what if they each live on their own side of the duplex? They could be together or apart as much as they would like. After years of things not working out, the house was ours in a matter of weeks. It wasn't even listed on the market.

Now my mom lives on one side, and Tina lives on the other. They are happy together. They are together in their own way. They love each other, and never in a million years would I have thought that I would be the one to keep them that way. I have no doubt that I was led to that solution by God and things fell into place by His hand. I have no doubt that He is mindful of my mom and Tina. A perfect solution was created for them. Both of them. Does it make sense? Is it normal? Is it easy to explain? No. But they are both my moms, and I love them. Even if it took me way too long to show it.

I am sure by this point in the book you are wondering what my stance is on homosexuality and The Church of Jesus Christ of Latter-day Saints.

I am not going to pretend to be a prophet or an apostate. I am not going to act like I have answers that no one else really seems to have about why people are gay or exactly what will happen with the Church's policy or God's judgment in the eternities. I lived a life of black and white, and it led me down a dark path. I thought I had the answers to everything. Now I realize how little I actually know.

The thing I do know is that as a fully believing, temple-attending, prophet-sustaining, daily-scripture-reading Latter-day Saint and a son of a lesbian, I have come to see how hard it is for the LGBTQ+ community to find their place in the world, and especially in the Church, over the years.

Can you imagine how hard it would be to attend a church that doesn't consider your marriage, your love, or your feelings and actions to be appropriate in the sight of God yet feel like you were given those feelings by God at birth? Can you imagine the thoughts of inadequacy that accompany a young man or woman with same-gender attraction as they go on a mission to serve the Lord? Yet there are many who attend church and serve missions and do the best with the life they have been given, whether they are active members, excommunicated, or temple-recommend wielding. That to me is mighty like the faith of early Latter-day Saint pioneers, who walked the plains to find their Zion. It flies in the face of popular culture and the world, yet it happens in congregations and communities across the world.

I also completely understand why many in the LGBTQ+ community would choose to have no affiliation whatsoever with the Church. Many have not been able to find a safe place or feel true love and support from family and Church members. It breaks my heart. I ask myself this: What if the roles were reversed, and being in a straight relationship wasn't acceptable in the eyes of God? What if the feelings I had for women and the love I have for my wife were considered wrong? Would I still be able and willing to be part of the Church based on my own feeling about revelation that has come to me? Would I still be able to live the teachings? Would I still be able to find love for myself and understand the love God has for me? I have had a hard enough time with my own personal struggles. If I had to add my sexuality on top of that, I don't know what I would do. For that fact alone, I pray that all of us will do more to help, support, and accept the choices that our gay family and friends make, whether the path is in or out of the Church. Life is hard enough without our judgments holding others back.

I do still wish more than anything that my mom would feel comfortable coming to church with my family. I would love for people to learn from her kindness and tolerance for all. I would love for her to learn from the challenges that others go through. I would love for her to be able to expand her group of friends to a congregation full of people that all fall equally short in the eyes of God and need to rely on the Savior's Atonement. But I no longer wish that she weren't gay in order to do it. I also completely understand why she stays home each Sunday while my family gets ready and goes to church. I hope I live to see the day when she will feel comfortable coming as an open lesbian yet still feel true love and support from the congregation . . . and me. I know she already feels love from God and is just waiting for the rest of us to catch up.

One of my favorite parts of the Book of Mormon is found in Mosiah 18. Alma had taken a group of people into the wilderness and stepped into the waters of Mormon and asked:

> As ye are desirous to come into the fold of God, and to be called his people, and are willing to bear one another's burdens, that they may be light;
>
> Yea, and are willing to mourn with those that mourn; yea, and comfort those that stand in need of comfort, and to stand as witnesses of God at all times and in all things, and in all places that ye may be in, even until death, that ye may be redeemed of God, . . .
>
> Now I say unto you, if this be the desire of your hearts, what have you against being baptized in the name of the Lord, as a witness before him that ye have entered into a covenant with him, that ye will serve him and keep his commandments, that he may pour out his Spirit more abundantly upon you? (Mosiah 18:8–10)

Alma's followers did desire, and they did get baptized. I am a baptized, believing member of the same church, and that means this statement stands for me just as much as it did for them. I need to be willing to bear others' burdens, mourn with those that mourn, comfort those that stand in need of comfort, and stand as a witness of God at all times and in all things.

I can't think of anyone I need to do all of it for more than my mother and every other person who feels judgment and the absence of love from Church members. I need to do better. I have been part of the problem. But I am learning, and I want to be part of the solution. It took my own crisis of faith, depression, lessons of patience, and new understanding of revelation to be humble enough to open my mind and heart to truly understand others' struggles. I want to show them the support they deserve. I pray that others don't have to go through the same rocky road and roller coaster of a life that I did and can learn from my experiences instead.

CHAPTER 8

Finding My Father

MY GOOD FRIEND ED AND I were talking at a conference when he asked me about my family. When I told him that I had never met my father, and more importantly, my father didn't even know about me, his jaw dropped, and in a way that only Ed could, he gave me advice that I couldn't shake.

"You know, Mike, twenty-something Ed was very different from forties Ed. I was just crazy enough that there is a good chance that there are little Eds running around the country somewhere that I don't know about. I would want to know, because . . . well, they are little Eds."

Despite the fact that he was trying to make me laugh, he also made a valid point that I hadn't thought about. As a father, my dad had the right to know that he had a son. At the same time, I worried that telling him would either (1) upset his life and family, if he had one, or (2) upset my mom or my family if it didn't go well.

So I did what anyone would do and stalked him online to try to learn what I could. I typed his name into Google and clicked search. I went to images and found his picture. It completely shocked me to see that the caption said he was splitting time between Utah and the United Arab Emirates. I clicked it before thinking. It took me directly to his LinkedIn profile, and I practically screamed out loud before the page finished loading.

As a marketer, I should have known better, but I was so caught up in the moment that I didn't even think about the fact that when you click on a LinkedIn profile, the person you view can see that you were on their profile.

So there would be a nice picture of Mike Ramsey from Burley, Idaho, on a list that he could see the next time he logged in.

That's right, I accidentally let my father know I was stalking him. Well-played, detective Mike. Within three days I received the following email.

Dear Mr. Mike Ramsey;

How are you. My name is Sied I got a message that you looked at my professional profile (LinkedIn). I hope you liked what you saw, but excuse my question if you do not mind, are you related to Janet Ramsey of Burley, ID if you are how is she doing? She is a friend from Utah State University.

I could hardly believe what I was reading. I tipped him off, he totally caught on, and he had reached out! At this point, I don't think he had any idea that I was his son. But he knew I was Janet's. I had no idea how to respond. I wasn't ready to divulge any information about my true intention of looking him up, so I settled on a version of the truth. I wrote him back.

She is doing great! Still lives in Burley, along with the rest of her family. I was talking to her about Utah State times a while back, and she brought you up. I asked where you were now, and she had no idea, so I looked you up. Hope your life is well.

He wrote a basic email back, and I avoided a serious encounter that I was not ready for at that time.

As the months continued to roll by, I couldn't shake the fact that the interaction was left unresolved. I hadn't responded. I also couldn't shake the feeling that I needed to let him know more.

After five months of sitting on it, I went to my mom and told her it was time to let him know. She looked at me for a minute, nodded, and told me that she would write him and let him know first, so that any of his questions wouldn't initially be directed toward me. It was a selfless act, and one that I was truly grateful for.

The letter was hard.

It explained why she did what she did and is personal enough that I have decided it's one of the few things that I will not share, simply out of respect for them both.

Regardless of the reasons, the fact of the matter was that thirty-plus years ago I was born, and my dad had just found out. I didn't know what his reaction would be. I was completely excited and definitely scared. I checked my email every ten minutes, day after day, hoping that there would be some type of message that would answer the questions I was dying to know.

As time went on with no word, I figured that the news had not gone over well, and I gave up on hearing from him.

I still didn't have a father. But I figured that wouldn't stop me from being a good father to my children. So we loaded up our van and made the long drive to the most magical place on earth: Disneyland.

You might remember what happens next. I was sitting on a little white boat, "It's a Small World" playing over and over like a broken record, spewing happiness on all within earshot, when my phone vibrated and I looked down to see an email from my father, who, this time around, knew he was writing his son.

/////

I spent a lifetime contemplating what it would be like to carry on a conversation with my father. I never thought it would have been brought about by an accidental view of a LinkedIn profile. I also didn't imagine it would be through email. But there I was reading a few paragraphs about his life, his experience with my mom, and his desire to come back from the United Arab Emirates to be closer to his family in Utah. Through the messages, I could tell like he seemed like a good man. Someone trying to do the best given his circumstances, and definitely trying to handle this earth-shattering news.

How'd the conversation go?

It felt surprisingly normal. Like hearing from someone you haven't seen in a very long time. The hardest part was knowing what to say after the initial data points on life were shared about the number of kids we've each had and places we've lived. I simply didn't know what more to say, and neither did he. The result was that I didn't say much of anything. Our email communication happened, initial pleasantries were shared, and then silence.

I initially thought that reaching out would change everything. Funny enough, as quick as the conversation took place, things went back to normal as if the event hadn't happened at all.

Now, at this point you might think that this has the potential to be the greatest letdown ever written. You might have expected me to tell you the story of some amazing meet-up in the Middle East where I learned interesting things about him, his culture, and his religion. Or it could have been written that we met up in some total dive diner in Utah where a lady named Barb brought my father and me pancakes and scrambled eggs while we caught up on years lost.

I know that is how I thought things were going to play out. Deep down it might even have been what I wanted. It would have made for a better story, stellar chapter, and potentially a Lifetime channel movie for the midafternoon audience. But it's not the reality of what happened.

After a few back-and-forth points of communication, it was done for the time being.

As I have reflected on how things played out since that first contact, I came to a very simple conclusion. I needed him to know that I existed. It was his right. But though I always wanted a father, I didn't *need* one.

Growing up fatherless was hard. Explaining that my dad was Middle Eastern and that is why I have curly dark hair and super tan skin dropped a lot of jaws in Burley when people would ask who my dad was. But I had the help of two moms. Others stepped in when and where they could, but ultimately there was one Father who I learned to lean on the most. I could talk to Him constantly and hold back nothing. Though there were plenty of times we didn't have the best of relationships, it always seemed to eventually work out.

The father I really *needed* all along was my Heavenly Father.

It seemed like I had spent a lifetime searching to fill the void, and every step simply brought me closer to knowing and understanding Him. I prayed, I read, I lived, and between it all my soul was always trying to be one with my Father in Heaven and understand the messages and revelations He was constantly sending me. Little by little, through the events I shared in the book, along with countless left unshared, I have come to know, believe, and trust in Him.

As of now, I still haven't communicated with my biological father beyond those initial introductions and basic series of questions. I don't know if the day will come when more happens and the Middle East trip or Barb's Diner in Utah plays out. There is one line in the very first email he shared that summed things up quite well for both of us, though. He wrote:

I would have loved to be part of your life while you were growing up, but it was never meant to be.

For some reason, my life was as it was. A son of a lesbian and a Muslim who didn't know he had a son. All so that I could have the experiences I needed to know God and my purpose. Also, so that I could appreciate the opportunity I have to be a father myself. I am better for it.

CHAPTER 9

Finding My Future

AS OF TODAY, I AM THIRTY-FIVE years old. I have said to some that I feel like I jammed enough experiences into my first thirty-odd years to last a lifetime. Deep down, though, I know that things are just warming up.

I have no idea what the future holds beyond a few bits and pieces from flash moments of revelation that may or may not play out as I expect. But I can say with confidence that I am excited.

So how does one find their future? The answer is simple. They learn from their past and live in the present. So what have I learned up to this point?

Mostly, I have learned over the years of good, bad, awkward, and heated conversations with loved ones that religion and homosexuality are hard subjects. The only thing harder than talking about either . . . is living them. Yep. That's right. Both have it really, really hard. Since I can only claim to have lived one side of the equation and observed the other from a close view, I am going to share my thoughts from that perspective.

Having it easy was never part of any religion's doctrine that I have ever heard of. Usually it was just the opposite.

Like when Jesus said:

But love ye your enemies, and do good, and lend, hoping for nothing again. (Luke 6:22)

Not every one that saith unto me, Lord, Lord, shall enter into the kingdom of heaven; but he that doeth the will of my Father which is in heaven. (Matthew 7:21)

Or Mohammad:

Be sure. We shall test you with something of fear and hunger [or] some loss in goods or lives or the fruits (of your toil) but give glad tidings to those who patiently persevere. (Qur'an 2:153–57)

Or Buddha:

However, many holy words you read, however many you speak, what good will they do you if you do not act on upon them?

As mentioned in previous chapters, my confidence in who I was and my relationship with God dramatically blossomed when I read the Book of Mormon and Bible. I have continued to gain a deeper relationship as I have lived and learned more of the teachings and simply lived life. The times I have learned the most were when it was hard. Really hard. But, like all hard things, it has made me who I am and ultimately has given me strength. Here are the hardest lessons I have learned that will be a guide for my future and hopefully yours:

EVERYBODY THINKS THEIR OWN THINKING IS RIGHT. WHAT WE ALL NEED TO BE IS EMPATHETIC.

I have had very few conversations with people who thought that their religion or way of life is false or wrong. On the other hand, I have had thousands of conversations with people who would argue or even fight for their beliefs. I sometimes do the same because my beliefs are . . . well, mine. They are part of me. I earned them through a life of learning, and funny enough, others feel exactly the same about their beliefs. I have yet to meet a person who bluntly says, "You know, I think the things I believe about life, religion, politics, and the pursuit of happiness are total crap. Can I have your beliefs on those things?"

I shared some of my first arguments about religion in previous chapters. Many were with my mom. We agree on so much, other than politics and religion, which just happen to be the two things that separate friends and families and have been the causes of a majority of the wars across our world's history.

When I left on my mission to England, I kept thinking that if my own mom was so firmly against my beliefs, then how would I ever find others who would listen? What I found over two years was that not a single person I talked to and argued with about points of doctrine was converted . . . or talked to us again. Or smiled at us.

On the other hand, people who did become converted were already looking for something, and the doctrine we taught them simply made sense and aligned with their basic belief system about life. I never once convinced someone of the error of their ways. No amount of scripture memorization or logic worked if they thought their way was right.

The problem then is when we cannot accept that it is okay for others to believe things that are different than, or in opposition to, our beliefs.

Nowhere is this more apparent than in conversations about the Church versus homosexuality. Many people on both sides want 100 percent surrender from the other. What I want is for people to put themselves in the others' shoes.

If you are gay, try to understand why Latter-day Saints believe what they believe and the rich history and good lives many have had by following that belief system. Accept that *they* believe in the Book of Mormon, in its teachings, and that God works through a prophet on earth today the same way He did through all of the scriptures. Accept that the current Latter-day Saint teachings from the family proclamation state that marriage between a man and a woman is ordained of God. They can believe this and still love you. You do not have to like it. You don't have to agree. But you can offer them the same thing you desire, which is the freedom to choose what to believe.

If you are a Latter-day Saint, try to put yourself in the shoes of someone who is gay, so you can understand the hurt and exclusion and persecution so many have experienced. I'm going to let you all in on a little secret. Neither side is going to change their core beliefs by argument or force. Instead, understanding and acceptance will come for both when we put our pride aside and learn to love our neighbors as much as we love ourselves and our own ideas. My hope is that I can be a voice in the middle. I'm proud to be a Latter-day Saint, and I'm proud to have a lesbian for a mother. It has taken me a lifetime to get to the point I am at, but I accept and am finally at peace with the contradictions between the two without having all the answers right now. Can you do the same?

NOBODY'S PERFECT.

But their scribes and Pharisees murmured against his disciples, saying, Why do ye eat and drink with publicans and sinners?

And Jesus answering said unto them, They that are whole need not a physician; but they that are sick.

I came not to call the righteous, but sinners to repentance. (Luke 5:30–32)

There have been many times when I have been offended by or have offended someone at church or in life. When I was around fourteen, I went on a Young Men camping trip to Island Park. I didn't really attend church too often at that time and was extremely hesitant to go.

I was joking around with a few of the boys and got a little loud and rowdy. The bishop at the time got right in my face with his finger and told me to shut up and be quiet because there were other people in the area. It was sharp, it was fierce, and it made me instantly not like the man and want to go home. I had enough daddy issues at the time to already be a little hesitant around authoritative men, and it took me a long while before I went back to a church meeting with my grandparents.

Church leaders since Adam (remember the apple?) have made mistakes or have done things that people find offensive or simply don't understand. Our Church history is filled with examples that have caused people to leave or doubt, and who can blame them?

People make mistakes, and those mistakes can hurt others. I have heard one too many horror stories of how Church leaders were too fierce, said the wrong thing, or didn't say enough, and left pieces of people's souls in the crossfire. I have also heard stories of how hard some have been on leaders who are just trying to do their best. Guess what? Nobody is perfect. The hard part is learning to forgive.

> For if ye forgive men their trespasses, your heavenly Father will also forgive you. (Matthew 6:14)

> I, the Lord, will forgive whom I will forgive, but of you it is required to forgive all men. (D&C 64:10)

The worst feeling I've have ever had was hatred or contempt for someone who hurt me or someone I love. It's bitter, it's hard, it's prideful, and it stops us from moving forward. On the flip side, loving others is the best feeling I have ever had. To love others, we have to accept that they are not perfect and that we aren't either. People sin. It's what we do. It's like sugar: we all know that it can be bad for us, but at the end of the day it just tastes so good. So we eat it. Sin is the same. We know what's right, and we fall short for various reasons. Church isn't for perfect people with perfect lives and perfect families. It's for people who are offensive, offended, angry, sad, prideful, shameful, depressed, poor, rich, addicted, or afraid. We need to accept each other and where we each are at in our journey. More importantly, we need each other.

We also need to simply be a little more genuine about ourselves and admit our mistakes, shortcomings, and weaknesses. For instance, a long time ago it was fairly common in the Church to hear things like, "Don't talk about your past sins or transgressions." I always wondered where this came from, and the only reference I could find was in *Teaching, No Greater Call* and specifically referred to comments while teaching a class. But that manual was discontinued, and that phrase didn't make it into *Teaching the Savior's Way*, which was the updated LDS Church manual for teachers.

Around the same time the new teaching manual came out, the Church started publishing a plethora of videos of real people with real problems and how they deal with them and overcome others.

Culturally, though, many took the initial idea of keeping past transgressions out of lessons plans and extended it into every part of their public persona. They took on covering or hiding their sins and weaknesses and put on a mask for a sense of perfection. I know I have been guilty of this over the years. Instead of being honest with others about the struggles I was facing with depression, sin, fear, and doubt, I would smile and tell everyone things were great. In reality, I was hurting inside. I felt like I was the only one who was going through difficult times.

Imagine if we were genuinely honest in our church gatherings. If speakers, teachers, and class members opened themselves up more and shared what was really going on in their lives, what would that do to Latter-day Saint congregations and people who are visiting?

There was a study done at Google called Project Aristotle to determine what made employee groups successful versus those that struggled. In my mind, the same things that would motivate people to work well together at a company would work in the Church, and I found the outcome of the study to be very applicable. Project Aristotle found the most important ingredient for success was psychological safety—the idea that team members feel safe to take risks and be vulnerable in front of each other, and that no one would embarrass or punish another for admitting a mistake, asking for help, or offering ideas.[2]

Do you feel like you can do that with your friends and in your congregation?

I didn't for a long time. Then I decided to open up. I shared the hardest stories from my life in classes, from the pulpit, and in conversations, and I would have people afterward come to me and thank me because they were going through something

---

2   re:Work, Google, https://rework.withgoogle.com/print/guides/57213126 55835136/.

similar and they didn't know who to talk to about it. All it took me was several seconds of radical courage and faith to share, and then the floodgates began to open for others to do the same. Why? Because they began to feel safe, knowing that others were battling similar things as well. Others weren't perfect.

My sincere hope in publishing this book is that by shedding light on my journey and the deepest, darkest corners of my soul, it will help others to do the same.

My fear and shame have been diminished with every keystroke and completed word, and it feels great. I want that same experience for everyone and will spend the remainder of my life being a genuine voice helping people realize that, for the most part, everyone is doing the best they know how. We all fall seriously short of perfection. It's part of the plan for us, and it's my belief that we need to rely fully on the Savior because our own strength is infinitely insufficient without Him.

SOMETIMES YOU JUST HAVE TO HAVE FAITH.

I've shown in chapter after chapter that I am not a patient man. I pay for the fastest internet I can get in Burley, Idaho (which still falls extremely short of my expectations). I avoid lines at any cost. I even paid three times the price at Legoland in Germany to skip the long wait times, and I never regretted it. I pay extra for next-day delivery. I skim emails to get to the important parts. I like to be in control of my time, and waiting for something to happen is extremely hard for me. Waiting is an act of faith. When you wait, you are showing that you have faith that something or somebody will come and end your wait. You simply have hope for the future.

It's now been ten years since I had the very specific revelation about being called to serve as a bishop. To this day it is still a mystery why the revelations came and why I felt the way I did.

What I can say is there is not a day that goes by that I don't think about it. Ten years is a long time, and it hasn't gotten easier. But I have learned that I can continue to have faith and hope that the revelation was real and served a purpose that someday I will understand. Or I can doubt it and struggle with the feelings of fear or despair and doubt that God is real and can speak to His children. I have done both. I have felt that I was wrong or God was wrong. I have doubted all that has been revealed to me and tried to forget it. But when I decide to accept that I am not in control and have to wait for the answers, I feel at peace. I can see life more clearly. I can be patient.

We all have questions. We all have major failures, and I would go as far as to say we all have traumatic events that transpire in our lives and leave us with very little hope and understanding. The answers might not come for years. They might not come for twenty years. To be honest, they might not come in this life. The question is if you can take a step into the dark without knowing what you will find.

For instance, after all the research, struggle, politics, and religious thoughts on homosexuality, has anyone ever been able to give a truly adequate answer on why someone is gay?

One of my favorite unsung heroes is a man by the name of Oliver Granger. He was a friend of Joseph Smith's and was given the impossible task of settling debts and issues in Kirtland, Ohio, after the bulk of the membership left and headed to Missouri. In a revelation for him in Doctrine and Covenants 117, he was told:

"When [you] fall, you shall rise again, for [your] sacrifice shall be more sacred unto me than [your] increase."

The Lord told him it was okay to fall, to fail. He basically let him know in advance that the mission was hard and he would have to contend earnestly. Oliver spent the rest of his life trying to accomplish what was asked of him, and he was largely unsuccessful in selling the Church's property.

I can only imagine the level of patience he had. The interesting part of the story for me is that he was told his sacrifice was more sacred to the Lord than his success. Sacrifice is the outcome of tested patience. It leads to the development of faith, hope, and then charity, which is the highest, noblest, strongest kind of love. To me, developing that kind of love for God and people is worth the wait. Maybe the reason the Church versus homosexuality is even a thing is for us all to learn a little love and patience as we wait for more revelation.

LIFE IS ABOUT CHANGE.

When I was a missionary, I lived with ten companions in six different cities in two years. It was constant change. As soon as I got to know people in a given city and developed close friendships, I would be asked to move and start the process over from scratch. It wasn't easy. But every experience taught me new things and kept me from getting complacent and comfortable. I came home feeling like I had lived a full life's worth of ups and downs in two years.

I have also had roughly fifteen different responsibilities in the Church since I have been home from my mission. I have spent time teaching classes to adults, college students, and seven-year-olds. I have been an executive secretary to the bishop, a stake Young Men president, a ward clerk, a website builder, a camp director, and many other things.

Each unique responsibility has impacted my life and taught me different lessons about service, love, patience, organization, public speaking, and empathy. The list could go on and on. Very few times in a calling, or as a missionary, did I want change, but I have come to realize that I am better because of it. Don't be afraid to try something new, for variety is the essence of life. Diverse experience has helped me to see from other perspectives and, most important, has shown me that we are all equal. We all have times to shine, times to support, and times to sit in the shade.

One thing that I find fascinating is the root meaning of repentance, which is simply to change. I always looked at repentance as something you only did when there were really big mistakes. Instead, I have come to realize that life is one big repentance process from the beginning to the end. It's constant and continuous. In the wise words of my mission president, "He who rests, rusts."

My views on homosexuality, my mother, and my religion have dramatically changed over the years. I embrace that change and learn more with every step. Don't rust in your ways. Always seek further light and knowledge that can help you grow to love deeper and see more.

"NOT MY WILL, BUT THINE, BE DONE."

As the Savior knelt on bended knee in the Garden of Gethsemane, surely feeling overwhelmed at the task ahead of Him, He said:

Father, if thou be willing, remove this cup from me: nevertheless not my will, but thine, be done. (Luke 22:42)

Nothing on this earth has ever been harder for me than giving my will away to another freely. The Savior did just that and, while grasping tree and stone, drank from the bitter cup of all the sins, shortcomings, fears, death, and guilt that mankind had experienced and rose above them all.

I like doing what I want to do. I don't like being told what to do. Being humble enough to pray and turn yourself over to God while spending your days doing what He would want you to do is the ultimate sacrifice we can make in this life. Our will is truly the only thing that can't be taken away from us. It has to be given away freely, and the ability to choose that path is ours.

I can't count the times I have felt like I should stop and help someone, or stand up for others, or get down on my knees and pour my soul out to God, but instead I did something I wanted to do. I think it takes a lifetime to learn to truly submit to God's will in all things, but as I have watched and witnessed those who do, it seems they are the ones that truly have found themselves and their life's purpose.

I think the Prophet Joseph Smith said it best:

I am like a huge, rough stone . . . ; and the only polishing I get is when some corner gets rubbed off by coming in contact with something else, striking with accelerated force . . . all hell knocking off a corner here and a corner there. Thus I will become a smooth and polished shaft in the quiver of the Almighty.[3]

My dad is a Muslim who I barely know. My mom is a lesbian who has loved me dearly, and it took me years to offer her that same love in return. I'm a believing Latter-day Saint because I read, I pray, and I continue to feel and see my Heavenly Father work in my life.

---

3 *Teachings of the Prophet Joseph Smith*, sel. Joseph Fielding Smith [1976], 304.

It's been terrifically hard yet absolutely exciting. I've experienced deep depression and overwhelming joy. I've been the harshest of critics and an absolute believer. Through the extremities of it all, I have learned that the reason I do what I do, the reason I wrote this book, is to do God's will. I want to be a little more like Him. That is what brings me peace and happiness. The conundrum is that I came into this world with my own ideas, a healthy dose of intolerance, a long list of shortcomings, and enough stubbornness to try and stop water from flowing down a hill. But through it all, God has been patient with me. In turn, I have started being patient with myself as I try each day to align with Him. That is the ultimate lesson from my past that will help me find my future. I hope that, despite all of my imperfections, I can spend the rest of the time I have allotted on this earth learning to say, "Not my will, but my Heavenly Father's, be done."

ACKNOWLEDGMENTS

THERE WAS A PLETHORA OF FOLKS who pushed this work along from the point where it was barely legible to something I am truly proud of. While I don't have the space to mention you all by name, there is a fairly decent chance you will make it into my will. Thank you.

A few folks need to have special thanks mentioned. Simply because the amount of influence they have had on the work and the story is too great not to mention.

First, to my mom. I was scared to death to have you read the manuscript. Thank you for understanding my need to share and for the hug you gave me after you read it.

To Hillary, my dear wife. Thank you for constantly pushing me to write and letting me know when it was awful, okay, or wonderful.

To Branson, Wendy, Kurt, Louise, Jacque, and Aaron. Your feedback was crucial and changed things for the better.

To Al. You opened the door on being genuine and showing me that people wanted to hear a good story. You helped my book find a home, and your feedback was fantastic. May you continue to be the leader you were born to be.

To the Cedar Fort crew—Bryce, Kathryn, Nicole, Kim, Wes, and others. I know I've been a royal pain. Thank you for dealing with my craziness to bring this book to those who need to read it.

To my Heavenly Father. Thank you for giving me a story worth sharing.

Lastly, to you, the reader. Thank you for taking a chance on my story. I hope you found something on the pages worth sharing.

ABOUT THE AUTHOR

MIKE RAMSEY IS AN AWARD-WINNING SPEAKER and writer on subjects ranging from learning hard lessons in life to building and surviving business ventures. His marketing and investment company, Nifty Ventures, has been recognized by *Inc.* as one of the fastest-growing private companies in America. Mike is married to his lifelong crush, and they have at least four children, depending on when you are reading this. He is active in his church and never quite active enough on a treadmill. You can follow Mike's next adventure or see if he can come and tell a crowd about it at MikeRamsey.org.

Scan to visit

MikeRamsey.org